INNER REWILDING

A Scientist's Journey Into Being

HOLLY ERIN COPELAND

Copyright © 2026 by Holly Erin Copeland

All rights reserved. No part of this publication may be reproduced, distributed or transmitted in anyform or by any means without permission of the publisher, except in the case of brief quotations referencing the body of work and in accordance with copyright law.

The information given in this book should not be treated as a substitute for professional medical advice; always consult a medical practitioner. Any use of information in this book is at the reader's discretion and risk. Neither the author nor the publisher can be held responsible for any loss, claim or damage arising out of the use, or misuse, of the suggestions made, the failure to take medical advice of for any material on third party websites.

Cover art: Ragana Design

ISBN 978-1-916529-54-0 Paperback
ISBN 978-1-916529-55-7 Ebook

The Unbound Press
www.theunboundpress.com

Praise for Holly Erin Copeland

Holly's book reads like a conversation with a trusted friend who shares the wild wisdom gained on her long journey from despair to a precious return to the home within. It is a beautifully written story that will help support many on their own journey. A compass for the most important journey of all.

Ian Haycroft, founder of *Theclearmindway* and
The Wisdom Path Project

As a trained scientist and a heart-centered explorer, Holly bridges the gap between scientific proof and intuitive felt experience. This book is a powerful synthesis of current research and ancient practices to show that we are inextricably woven together, inseparably one with all of life—and that recovering our lost sense of connection is paramount right now. Holly presents her thesis in the context of her own profound journey of healing, which inspires us to investigate and test the implications of this paradigm shift for ourselves. What if we view every illness and crisis as an opportunity to learn, expand, and explore? Holly leaves us with the hope that, by doing so, maybe it is possible to heal ourselves and our planet from the inside out. As a practitioner and teacher of meditation and holistic fitness for over forty years, I am thrilled to see such a testament to the truth and efficacy of these insights and practices.

Kevin Schoeninger, Co-Founder and Director of
RaisingOurVibration.net

Hey unbound one!

Welcome to this magical book brought to you by The Unbound Press.

At The Unbound Press we believe that when women write freely from the fullest expression of who they are, it can't help but activate a feeling of deep connection and transformation in others. When we come together, we become more and we're changing the world, one book at a time!

This book has been carefully crafted by both the author and publisher with the intention of inspiring you to move ever more deeply into who you truly are.

We hope that this book helps you to connect with your Unbound Self and that you feel called to pass it on to others who want to live a more fully expressed life.

With much love,
Nicola Humber

Founder of The Unbound Press

www.theunboundpress.com

*To my beloved daughters, Mia and Abby,
whom I love beyond all measure.*

*And to every being working tirelessly
for the benefit of humanity and Planet Earth.*

Contents

Foreword by Stephen Altair	xiii
Preface	xv
Part I: Tracing My Way Back	**1**
1. For the Love of Wilderness	3
2. The Bottom of the Well	15
3. Down the Rabbit Hole	27
4. The Wound is Where the Light Enters	39
5. Polishing the Heart Clean	49
6. Breathing into Coherence	65
7. Attuning to the Vibrational Universe	79
8. Love, Rewilded	91
9. Falling in Love with the World	99
Part II: The Path and Practices of Inner Rewilding	**105**
10. Maps and the Medicine Wheel of Inner Rewilding	107
11. Awaken to Peace	111
12. Attune to the Living Universe	121
13. Allow the Flow	137
14. Align to Your Wild Heart	149
15. Homecoming	159
Acknowledgments	165
Resources for Inner Rewilding	169
About the Author	173

*"The future enters into us,
in order to transform itself in us,
long before it happens."*

– Rainer Maria Rilke

Foreword

It is with great reverence that I introduce *Inner Rewilding*—a truly remarkable journey of embodying this Earth and her power from my dear friend Holly Erin Copeland.

We first met years ago in a meditation group called *Raising Our Vibration*. Even then, Holly carried a rare presence—a fierce intellect paired with a deeply intuitive heart, a scientist who dared to ask the sacred questions and a willingness to traverse beneath the known, into the wilderness of consciousness, sound and healing that she so deeply loves exploring.

This book is the map of that wilderness, a record of her passage of healing, of stripping bare all that was not her own essential nature. Holly, like us all, believed in outward action as the savior of our world, until she realized, and documented, with exquisite honesty, the power that awakens when you allow the world to save you. Through dark meditation closets, icy rivers, plant medicine journeys and reconnecting to the world of the wilderness inside her, she reconnected to her own essential truth, the inner rewilding of the self.

What makes *Inner Rewilding* such an extraordinary book is that Holly points you back to yourself, to the mirror of yourself in all of nature, the nature that lies inside you. She guides you to trust the intelligence of your own body, and the wisdom of your own seasons in life. Her four principles—*Awaken to Peace, Attune to the Living Universe, Allow the Flow, Align to Your Wild Heart*— are lived truths, learned deeply in her own travels in life, both the inner ones and the outer journeys.

Holly's journey is an inner alchemy we can all relate to. She touches our own sense of remembrance. Her revelation is that *none of us are broken*. We've just forgotten how to listen to the wild, tender pulse of our hearts that already knows the way home.

To read *Inner Rewilding* is to sit beside a trusted guide through the cliffs and valleys of your own inner landscape. She makes you feel like your own deepest knowing is finally awake and ready for you to trust.

All of us, are being called back to our truth, the truth that has always lived inside us:

You are the wilderness you've been seeking.

With love and blessings,

Stephen Altair

Best Selling Author of Health Wealth and Wisdom in the New Millennium, Diary of a Yogi and Raising Our Vibration.

Preface

When this journey began, I was in my mid-forties. It was nuts, really. I owned a beautiful log home in Lander, Wyoming, with a loving husband, and together we were raising healthy twin girls who were high school soccer stars and at the top of their class. My job as Director of Science for a leading conservation organization was a dream come true. In my free time, I adventured around the world—rock climbing, canyoneering, and traveling to wild and remote places. And yet despite all this, something wasn't right.

My heart ached, overwhelmed by the sheer madness of our world—the way we treat animals, the environment, and each other. The little girl who wanted to save the whales and redwood forests when she was twelve had grown into a woman who dedicated her life to protecting our planet, but it wasn't enough. My mind had become an unruly tangle, crowded with questions I couldn't answer, and my body was quietly breaking down under the weight of a mysterious illness I couldn't seem to heal. Questions like:

What is the point?

Will my efforts ever be enough?

Is it possible to be happy amidst the ongoing planetary destruction—to not be crushed by the weight of all that's broken?

Do I even have a right to be happy?

I was lost.

All I knew was that I had to resolve the ache in my heart. While I'd spent the past 25 years working tirelessly to save the Earth, this time I knew I wouldn't find the answers I was seeking "out there." Instinctively, I knew I had to journey within. Even though I didn't really know what that meant, meditation seemed like the logical place to begin.

Like Alice, I fell down a rabbit hole as I immersed myself in indigenous and ancient wisdom and the frontiers of spiritual science. I spent countless hours practicing Kriya and Tibetan meditation, and nearly every other weekend sweating in a Native American sweat lodge. I trained in transformational breathwork, swam in icy rivers, and studied energy medicine and sound healing with tuning forks. I traveled to the jungles of Peru and Costa Rica to drink Ayahuasca. I did so many damn things.

There wasn't one single "awakening" moment, but rather a series of realizations that allowed the flame within my heart, which felt like it had almost been extinguished when I began, to gradually glow more brightly as I devoted myself to this path. Finally, years into the journey, the beauty of life was restored within me. The spark that I'd carried in my eyes as a young girl returned. I had fallen in love with myself, with life—and with the world again. And in that remembering, I came to understand that I didn't need to be fixed, nor did the world need to be fixed. I just needed to reconnect—not to the outside world, but within.

This was the journey of what I now call Inner Rewilding. In time, these realizations sparked a longing within me to help others find their way back to themselves, to the joy and love of being that is our birthright. This book is my way of honoring and sharing what I learned.

In retrospect, I realize I didn't truly know what self-love was, despite my decades on the spiritual path. I also didn't know what it meant to feel genuine belonging to the Earth, or what it was to feel deeply connected to myself and thus to all life—to feel that I really am part of everything I am aware of: the birds, rivers, forests, trees, and oceans.

It's not surprising, really, because we live in an analytical, left-brain-dominated world that has trained us to disconnect and separate. One that values control over intuition, productivity over presence, and transaction over relationship. We've inherited systems that reinforce an illusion of separation—between ourselves, nature, and the Divine.

This fundamental separation, the illusion that we are somehow apart from the living world and from the Source that animates it, is at the root of our suffering. The tragedies we see in the world today result from disconnection—from forgetting our unity and believing we are isolated fragments rather than expressions of the same sacred whole. The fractured and fragmented landscapes a collective mirror of how we feel on the inside.

For me, the word "wild" captures the essence of the wholeness and restoring the connection that we long for. Wild landscapes maintain the ecological connections and processes for plants and animals inhabiting them to migrate and thrive. They are very different from the managed and controlled landscapes that pervade our planet.

The story of the wolves returning to Yellowstone has lessons for us about wildness. As white settlers spread throughout North America, we extirpated them all. Then in 1980, something extraordinary happened. We decided to bring them back. And as they once again began to assume their apex role, we watched how the forests and meadows responded. The aspens and willows regenerated, the rivers changed course. We saw how the landscape and creatures suffered when we only wanted to accept some of the parts, and how everything flourished when wholeness was restored. What we thought we were managing by controlling it—removing what seemed dangerous, keeping only what was deemed useful—was actually slowly dying.

And just as the land can be made whole again, so can we.

To embrace wildness is to love and honor Nature on her terms—the inherent order, beauty and natural rhythms—without needing to control, tame and sanitize her. And we can learn to love ourselves the same way. We too begin to flourish when we stop trying to manage and control life and instead trust the deeper intelligence moving through us—

when we allow ourselves to feel with our hearts and follow what brings us alive.

If you've been feeling lost, uncertain, untethered, you're not alone. And you are not broken. We are living through a time of great unraveling, a time when so much of what we thought we could rely on is being called into question. Beneath the surface of that discomfort, something deeper is stirring—aching hearts called to remember and reconnect with who we truly are.

This book is not a step-by-step formula. It's not a rigid map. It's more like a compass—something to help you orient yourself, to point you back toward the truth that already lives inside you. In the first part of the book, I'll share my own story—the unraveling, the unexpected detours, and the path that slowly revealed itself. In the second part, I'll offer you four guiding principles of Inner Rewilding—insights and practices designed to help you awaken to your true nature, attune to the living universe, allow all parts within you, and align with your joyful heart.

The journey ahead isn't linear. It won't look the same for everyone. But its essence is universal: a turning inward. A reawakening of intuition and belonging. A reconnection to the living universe. A remembering of what it feels like to be joyfully human—equal parts free and deeply rooted.

This book is my offering to that remembering. It's part personal story, part guidebook, and most of all, it's a transmission of hope. Because I know what it's like to feel lost—to feel overwhelmed by the state of the world and unsure of how to keep going. I know what it's like to feel like you've tried all the things—achievement, activism, spiritual seeking—and still feel like something essential is missing. And I also know what it's like to find your way home.

I'm so honored that you are here, and wherever you find yourself—amidst the messiness, chaos, and uncertainty of life—know this: you are exactly where you're meant to be. You haven't missed your chance. You haven't taken a wrong turn. The answers you've been searching for aren't out there. They are within you.

PART I
TRACING MY WAY BACK

I
For the Love of Wildness

> *"It's not by accident that the pristine wilderness of our planet disappears as the understanding of our own inner wild nature fades."*
> *– Clarissa Pinkola Estes*

I was conceived in a tent under the stars. Mountains and trees were present from my earliest arrival on Earth, as though saying to me, "Come, beautiful human and drink in the splendor and magnificence of this sacred place. Feel its aliveness, its softness, its grandeur." Frequencies of soft pine duff and stars were imprinted within my cells, creating a destiny inextricably linked to the planet and its fate.

Planet Earth was my first guru, my teacher. Where others may be devoted to Christ, Krishna, or Mohammed, I first became devoted to what the indigenous people of South America call Pachamama, the spirit of our sacred planet Earth. Nature became my portal to the ineffable, transcendent and undefinable mystery of life.

Following this starry conception, I made my way into the world surrounded by nature even though I was born in the busy and urban Los Angeles basin. Whether playing beneath the weedy licorice in our backyard or searching for tadpoles in the mucky ponds of our neighborhood park, I was drawn to the outdoors.

My parents' strong connection to nature meant that our weekends and vacations were mostly spent backpacking and camping in the Sierras or exploring beaches along the wild Pacific Coast. I could scour tidepools for hours, reveling in awe at starfish and sea urchins clinging to lichen-covered rocks amidst the pounding surf. I was equally at home making my way by backpack beneath a canopy of Douglas fir and Ponderosa pines to summit some Sierra peak.

During winter, we didn't downhill ski at resorts like most of my friends. Rather, we were the oddball family at a Nordic ski area called Royal Gorge making our way on narrow "skinny" cross-country skis, my parents egging us on with promises of hot chocolate if we could make it to the little warming hut that lay miles in the woods. A typical teenager, I remember feeling annoyed that we were the "different family" and complaining to my parents about their choice to cross-country rather than downhill ski because it felt tiring and not as easy as lift skiing. But the beauty and solitude of winding through backcountry trails on skis would later turn into a passion and love that would develop through college and into adulthood.

At age 12, I went off to Camp Tawonga, a Jewish sleep-away camp near Yosemite National Park. For three glorious weeks, my days were filled with song, campfires, swimming, archery and making lanyards in the art barn under pine and oak trees. One year we backpacked in Yosemite to climb the backside of Half Dome up the ladders and chains. I was scared out of my mind—and it was the most exhilarating experience of my life so far. As far as I was concerned, camp was paradise.

The outdoor adventures continued into my teens when I traveled with a church youth group to Alaska. My family didn't belong to a church at the time, but my best friend Alison, whose family were members of the Episcopal church, said that the youth group was open to anyone. So, I promptly signed up because going to Alaska sounded like the most glorious and adventurous thing I could possibly dream of.

Off we went via ferry, train, and bus to Alaska to live in the tiny Athabascan village of Circle for two weeks to help finish a half-built church. I had a knack for making friends and striking up a conversation with one of the native Athabascan girls, which ended up in an invitation to visit her family's fish camp on the Yukon. During one indelible day, I helped the family carry out their summer routine. We checked and emptied salmon traps and hung fresh salmon from willows in stick-framed smokehouses.

At seventeen, I felt a strong urge to leave home for my junior year of high school and explore the world as an exchange student. As I reviewed the print catalog for the exchange student program, the tiny photos of the rugged Norwegian fjords coupled with the quaintness of the country pulled me in, and so at age seventeen, I left California for a year to live in Norway.

As it turns out, Norwegians are wild by nature. The sweet family I was assigned—the Rønningens—took me in like their own daughter, and I felt immediately at ease in their modest home perched on the edge of the Oslo fjord. They had an old cabin on a lake in the nearby woods only accessible by boat, so throughout summer and fall we would pack up the car for the weekend and then take a little motor boat out to the cabin where we would cook sausages and potatoes, wander through the forests and pick berries, and read.

That spring for Poska (Easter) week, which is as major a holiday as Christmas for Norwegians, we traveled to a postcard-idyllic Scandinavian "high mountain" hotel in the Rondane Mountains owned by family friends. During the day, we trekked out and skied the wide-open expanses beneath the southern mountains and in the afternoon came back to the most bountiful and delicious smorgasbord dinners that Scandinavians are famous for. Suddenly I felt grateful for my unusual childhood on x-country skis and saw that what had been unconventional and weird as an American teenager, was the most normal and conventional upbringing for a Norwegian.

In 1990 I set off into the Central Valley of California to study at the University of California at Davis. A contentious conservation issue of the time was an outcry over logging of the last of California's ancient old-growth redwood forests. Vehemently opposed to this logging, I joined a student environmentalist group inspired by the famed desert writer Edward

Abbey and the Earth First! movement and attended Deep Ecology talks and informal gatherings. Headed by David Orr, Earth First! was notorious for their unconventional methods of stopping logging, like pouring sugar in the engines of skidders. To my knowledge, our group didn't do those kinds of actions, but I found myself picketing old-growth logging on the shipping docks in Sacramento.

And then I read Edward Abbey's famous book *Desert Solitaire* and felt as though I'd finally found my tribe. A tireless advocate for wildness he wrote: "Wilderness is not a luxury but a necessity of the human spirit, and as vital to our lives as water and good bread. A civilization which destroys what little remains of the wild, the spare, the original, is cutting itself off from its origins and betraying the principle of civilization itself."

Abbey stirred in me a longing and deeper knowing about the value of wildness. Through Abbey I started to see that by taming Earth's wildness we betray the wildness within ourselves. Abbey took me back into the roots of nature and within him I found a kindred spirit and mentor for the value of wildness.

When spring break arrived, the student environmental group organized a desert trip to visit Ed Abbey's stomping grounds near Moab, Utah. In our student beater Subarus and Toyotas we explored back-country jeep trails and hiking trails of Arches and Canyonlands National Park.

At night we gathered around the campfire in folding chairs reading Abbey and talking about how to "save" the desert from the footprint of man's ever-increasing development of roads, transmission lines and oil and gas wells. Camping out under the starry cold desert skies cemented my passionate love and sense of belonging in the wild, deep red rock cliffs, canyons and wide-open landscapes of the Western desert.

Alongside Abbey, John Muir's poetic descriptions of the Sierras and celebrations of wilderness stirred my heart. Muir combined a deep appreciation for nature and wildness with the mystery of being human. He famously wrote: "The clearest way into the Universe is through a forest wilderness." Muir found himself and his place in the world through the mountains. With my own perinatal connection to mountains, reading Muir felt like coming home to myself.

Muir combined a passionate love for the wilderness with an ecological sense of the interconnectedness of all life. Everything he wrote made so much sense to me: "When one tugs at a single thing in nature, he finds it attached to the rest of the world." Muir saw nature as inextricably connected and existing as a web of life regardless of the appearance of seeming separateness as individuals—a tree, a leaf, a human.

The interconnected web of life isn't a new concept. Some version of this appears in most elementary school science classes, where the web of life is presented as a food chain—a hierarchy of organisms from smallest to largest, each consuming the next.

The story goes something like this: conifer forests create healthy soils that support earthworms; a robin eats the earthworm; a bull snake eats the robin; an eagle eats the bull snake; and when the eagle dies, she eventually decays back into the forest where the cycle begins again. I learned this story too, and it seemed both obvious and important. If we're all connected, then we'd better pay attention to all the components of the system. We can't eliminate one part and expect the whole to function well.

Yet somehow, our elementary school lessons seemed to be set aside or forgotten. Instead, my hopeful young heart struggled to reconcile what I was seeing: a mad race to burn, cut, farm, and pave every square inch of our beautiful planet, leaving acid rain, a depleted ozone layer, degraded soils, and deforestation in its wake.

And so, I did what any teenage rebel outraged by the actions of the so-called "adult" world would do. I became a fierce advocate for the environment, determined to become a warrior for the planet and fight to slow or halt the destruction. It was the only thing that made any sense looking out from my little view on the world. The one conceived under the stars pointed her compass towards what mattered most to her—nature—and went to work.

Fresh from my undergraduate education, I started as a fledgling geographic information systems (GIS) modeler for the US Forest Service. There I discovered that I had a knack for computer programming and a passion for wanting to understand the larger ecological story playing out on the landscape. GIS was the perfect marriage of these two, so just a few years later, I left the Forest Service to enter graduate school at the University of Wyoming and get further training in mapping and environmental sciences.

I was traveling around Wyoming as an eager graduate student as part of a NASA-funded grant program teaching teachers to use new hip (at the time) mapping software called ArcGIS in 1998, when an employee for The Nature Conservancy attended my workshop. She remarked how they could really use someone like me to help them map their conservation projects, which turned into a small mapping contract for them. I loved blending my technological skills and environmental passion to help guide their conservation work. The following year, just as I was completing my graduate degree, I could hardly believe my fortune when they offered me a permanent job as a mapping analyst and scientist at their state headquarters in Lander, Wyoming.

My husband, Scott, and I sold our home in Colorado and relocated to Wyoming, feeling incredibly blessed to call the small mountain town of Lander our new home. Lander lies at the base of the Wind River Mountains and is a crossroads of culture where artists, climbers, hunters, environmental advocates, and ranchers co-exist in a kind of mutual respect and appreciation for wildlife and open spaces. It was perfect for us.

We settled into our new community and the adventurous Western life in Lander. With winters often lasting six months, we adapted to the cold weather, grateful for our puffy down coats and all-wheel-drive Subaru that nearly everyone we knew owned. Summers were glorious with long sunny days that allowed us to camp, hike and fish on weekday evenings like we were living in a Sunset magazine feature article.

A few years later, our twin daughters, Mia and Abby, were born. Their arrival allowed us to fulfill our dream of raising children away from the chaos of the urban world—its strip malls and chain eateries. Instead, they grew up in the thriving town of Lander and the surrounding mountains.

They were Rocky Mountain girls, and we taught them everything we knew about mountain life. How to rock climb, backpack and hike in the mountains and not get lost, fly fish, cut and haul firewood, and hunt (and process) elk. They attended school with an eclectic blend of ranch kids, NOLS hipster kids, and Native American children from the nearby Wind River Indian Reservation. The nearest big city, Salt Lake City, was a five-hour drive across the sparse, high sagebrush desert—totally inconvenient for traveling anywhere, but offering protection from the crazy influences of city life. We had envisioned this modern-meets-rural life for them, and Lander more than delivered.

The busyness of raising two young children while working full-time kept my cup overflowing for the following ten years as my little babies grew into teenagers. I worked hard at my job, pouring my heart into the Conservancy—conducting research, writing papers, and traveling around the state giving talks. I was doing my best to balance a demanding career with trying to be a good mom and wife. It didn't feel "easy" by any means, but we were living the idyllic rural Western life, and in every respect by societal norms, my life was a "success."

For many years, this truly felt like the success it appeared to be. But gradually, something began to shift underneath the surface. A lifetime of buried hurts and unresolved questions began to surface from deep inside my heart. I just wasn't as happy as I used to be despite all the outward successes.

One night after a long day at work, I was standing in the kitchen at our large center island preparing dinner. Scott sat perched on a bar stool across from me. The girls were in the living room working on homework. I remember the tone of his voice and exact words as he said to me, "You just don't seem happy." Feeling resistance to his words, I fired back firmly, "What do you mean? I *am* happy," in a defensive tone. "I enjoy time with my friends, my work, my family. I'm happy [as though saying it a second time would make it more true]. What more do you want?" My wellbeing was suddenly on trial. After all I'd done to balance the demands of motherhood and career, I needed to achieve some perfect level of happiness too? It felt like an unfair expectation.

Looking back, though, his observation voiced something I knew deep down, even though it was painful to admit. Behind the curtain of my smiling face as mom, wife, and colleague, he was right. I wasn't truly happy. As much as I loved my family, friends, and work, the grind of life—all the doing and trying—was wearing me down. I was caught on a hamster wheel of doing, especially in my work as a conservation scientist where the environmental challenges felt insurmountable and continuous.

Honestly, it felt like nothing I did was ever enough. And behind that, an existential crisis was brewing. I needed answers to the bigger questions: "What's the point of all this striving?" and "Is this really what life is supposed to feel like?"

2

The Bottom of the Well

"In order to find our way, we must become lost."
– *Bayo Akomolafe*

My questions would soon find their answers, but not in the way I expected. First, I had to fall deeper into the despair that was already quietly consuming me. My work—the very thing I thought gave my life meaning—would pull me under, and my own body would begin to mirror the toxicity I saw everywhere in the world around me.

It's just past dawn and I am on Highway 287, headed to the University of Wyoming for a meeting with the team of migration scientists. As I come over a rise, two deer are lying dead in the middle of the road. My heart breaks open as I creep past them. They are a tremendous hazard where they are and could cause an accident, so I turn my car around and carefully park on the side of the road near them. It's a mother and a yearling side by side, and as I pull them by their feet, sliding their bodies gently off the road, I notice that they are still supple and warm. They've likely been killed in the pre-dawn only hours before.

Back in the car, tears stream down my face as the scent of deer rises from my hands. I cry not just for these creatures but for the needless carelessness of their deaths. I cry for the person who hit them and couldn't even take the time to stop and pull them to the side of the road.

After 23 years living in Wyoming, I'd seen way too many animals dead on the road. The worst are the ones still alive—suffering and helpless. And it's not just from cars. Trains are even more devastating. One of my biologist friends at the Wyoming Game and Fish Department once described an accident where a train hit a herd of pronghorn. Hundreds of them lay injured and dead along the tracks. Even now, just imagining the bloody, twisted aftermath triggers a deep welling ache of grief in my belly.

The pain of injured animals haunts me, but so does the loss of native grasslands and sagebrush to highly invasive plants, oil and gas drilling, and wind farms. Driving home on a beautiful May afternoon, my gaze rests uncomfortably on a sea of bright yellow leafy spurge crowding out the native sagebrush throughout the entire valley where I live.

Leafy spurge was first brought to North America as an ornamental plant from Asia in the mid-1900s. I'm sure it was brought here innocently, but spurge is particularly clever and casts thousands of seeds in early spring then infuses its underground environment with a milky nectar toxic to native plants. Spurge is so successful that it now occurs widely throughout the Western U.S., choking out millions of acres of native sagebrush and grasses.

I wish I could unknow what I know, but I can't. When I see hillsides of leafy spurge, I feel hopeless knowing the problem is way too big for underfunded local, state, and federal governments to tackle. Spurge is just one of many invasive plants slowly crowding out and replacing native habitats in the Western U.S.

If that wasn't bad enough, sagebrush is losing ground, not just to spurge but to human development: homes, oil wells, and wind farms. This fragmented patchwork makes it harder for wildlife to survive—especially species like the vulnerable and magnificent greater sage-grouse.

Populations of sage-grouse were once so numerous they darkened the skies. Now their numbers are a fraction of what they were. At the Conservancy, we study the effects of human development on vulnerable species like sage-grouse. We use computer models to show that if human development is reduced, populations will recover—and we must protect the best sage-grouse habitat for them to survive.

But neither the companies nor the State of Wyoming will curb development. So in compromise after compromise, the sage-grouse plan withers into a document filled with exceptions for industry so that in the end, development will mostly go on as usual. The sage-grouse saga has become yet another tale in my own heartbreak of grief for the environment. It feels like a horror movie that I can't turn off.

Revered ecologist Aldo Leopold once said: "One of the penalties of an ecological education is that one lives alone in a world of wounds." I too feel alone in a world of wounds where a simple drive home triggers all this pain. Pain for all the losses—the sagebrush lost to invasive species, sage-grouse to drilling, and deer to cars. The planet feels like a punctured artery draining too fast to heal. Beneath the surface of my work, a quiet despair simmers. Nothing feels "okay" at all. The hopelessness creates a sense of dread that feels like a dirty film covering a lens that I don't know how to clean.

This grief doesn't just feel personal—it feels ancestral, as though I was born into it. My ancestor Eugene Rogers from the 1800s was a fur trader who trapped sea otters in the Channel Islands off the coast of Santa Barbara. I have an old black-and-white photo of him standing beside a mountain of pelts. I wonder if I am here to repay that debt.

From the logging of old-growth redwood forests in college to my two decades with the Conservancy, the environmental issues keep coming, creating a well of despair within me that feels like it *has no bottom*. I sense an impossibility to escaping the mess that we've created—that there will never be enough time, money, or resources to end this planetary harm. This haunting sense of not-enoughness follows me everywhere, a hungry ghost I can't escape.

When impossibility rears its ugly head in one aspect of your life, it's bound to show up in another way—and in this case—literally *in my face*. God, the universe is so utterly ironic.

It all starts one very ordinary March morning. I wake up and head to the kitchen for my first cup of shade-grown bird friendly organic deliciousness. While it's brewing, I pad into the bathroom and as I'm washing my hands, glance casually into the mirror. Except this time, rather than seeing my usual somewhat scrunchy morning face, I notice a distinct and strange red puffiness under my eyes. That's odd, I think to myself as I stare intensely in the mirror wondering what might have caused this.

I am pretty careful with what I eat, drink and put on my body, always choosing organic minimally processed food and products with little to no chemicals. But it has to be something…I decide it's likely red wine, and abstain for the following week, but unfortunately, the same red puffiness under my eyes remains.

The following week, I leave for a work trip. As the trip progresses, the puffiness actually fades such that by the time I return home, incredibly it's gone. It feels amazing to be back to my normal self. I'm elated, but it turns out to be temporary because after just one night at home, the puffiness returns. For several months, the same pattern continues. The symptoms are present when I am home, but fade as soon as I travel away for a work trip. It doesn't take a rocket scientist to see the pattern. When I'm home, I'm sick. When I'm away, I am better. I become convinced that something in my home is making me sick.

At home, it's not just the facial symptoms. I feel exhausted too, and my face actually starts to worsen, the puffiness and redness travelling down my neck and upper chest too. I am desperate to know what is wrong. I spend countless hours Googling for answers, but all my searches just come up with more questions. I see my local doctor, who also appears quite stumped and while sympathetic has no explanation other than the possibility of an allergy to a product I'm using like laundry soap. He prescribes Prednisone and suggests that I add an antihistamine like Benadryl to alleviate my symptoms.

This pattern—and my frustration—continues for months with no clear answers until my dad connects me to Jeff, a family friend who is a retired physician and former leading U.S. environmental toxicologist. Jeff listens patiently to my story, asking detailed questions about my living environment and food intake, and finally offers his suspicion that I am suffering from mold exposure. *"Mold...really???"* I say, incredulous at his suggestion. We live in the high dry desert climate of the Rockies, so a mold issue honestly never crossed my mind. I am really surprised. Jeff suggests that I hire professionals to inspect our home for mold, as well get my urine tested. When I hang up the phone, I am both relieved and daunted at the implications.

The following day I schedule an appointment with my local naturopath to get myself tested and search for home mold specialists. The closest inspectors are in Denver six hours away and hiring them to come to Lander is cost prohibitive. Scott is an air quality specialist with decades of experience working with air samples, so we decide to purchase equipment to do our own mold testing.

Guided by our home mold tests, we find traces of mold in our den where spring rains had caused our basement to flood the previous year. We hire contractors to remove a portion of our newly installed bamboo wood floor. We also replace our front-loading washing machine, which I discover is on a list of appliances which have had mold problems. None of these solutions solves the problem though and my symptoms continue.

The urine test reveals extraordinarily high levels of certain types of mold in my system, confirming Jeff's suspicion. Months tick by as we search for the mold.

Finally, in October, the breakthrough comes. We'd spent the weekend in Yellowstone on a family camping trip. Like all other trips, the symptoms fade dramatically within 24 hours, only to come back in full force when I return home. Super frustrated by the resurgence of symptoms and racking my brain for answers, I discover an online article about mold in mattresses. That morning, I share with Scott that I think we need to buy a new bed. We'd already replaced so many items in our house that I'm sure he wasn't surprised.

A week later, my mom and her partner are visiting when the beautiful new organic wool bed arrives in the mail. Scott must disassemble the old bed to get it out of the bedroom, and to our complete shock, underneath the foam topper of the old bed which rests on an impermeable vinyl lining is a long layer of dark mold outlining each of our bodies. He shows it to me and we piece it together: years of sleeping on this mattress had caused the body heat to condense and form mold on the foam which had no way to breathe due to the vinyl. It's a horrendous design flaw. I am stunned in disbelief. All this time, the mold was literally right under my nose while I slept.

With the new bed in place and the mold source out of the house, I clean and air every soft item in the house with vinegar (as recommended by mold experts)—carpets, clothing, bedding (though I throw away our pillows). I feel like I'm home free, doing a little dance in my mind with relief at finally finding the source of the mold.

Or so I think.

Two weeks later, I am enjoying a simple Thai dinner with my family and 10 minutes into the meal, the mold symptoms return. My mind reels *"what is going on???"* with an inner cry of anguish. By this time, I had read enough on mold to suspect that the peanut sauce I was eating might have something to do with my symptom return. According to mold expert and biohacker Dave Asprey, who himself had mold poisoning, and filmed the movie "Moldy," peanuts are the moldiest food in our modern food system. The link seemed too obvious to ignore.

The next week, I eat tacos with corn tortillas and again the symptoms return. A little research reveals that corn is the second moldiest food in the US food system, and so that one quickly gets put on my "no eat" list, along with cheese and wine. I consult with Jeff and learn that my body has become hypersensitive to mold. He advises me to focus on detoxifying my body, starting with daily use of an infrared sauna.

The number of things I'm doing to clear mold from my body is starting to add up. I begin each day with a cocktail of supplements including glutathione, coconut charcoal, milk thistle, and hydrogen.

Inspired by a Bulletproof podcast, I decide to try coffee enemas, or as my biohacking friend Lindsey jokingly calls it: "upside down coffee." When I do it the first time, I feel awkward and uncomfortable—here I am in my bathtub, wondering how my wellness journey led me to this moment. The process involves holding warm coffee in my system long enough to be effective, but not so long that I can't make it to the toilet in time. I teeter between discomfort and relief, grateful when I complete the process successfully. Oh, the things I will do to feel better.

I've been reading a lot about the benefits of water fasting for detoxing the body. Lindsey is also a pro at fasting, so when I decide to do my first seven-day water fast to clean out and rebuild my system, I consult with her on the proper methods. The benefits of fasting are well-established within many traditions, including Ayurveda, helping the body reset and cleanse.

The first few days are brutal. As my body works to clear accumulated toxins and mold, I feel achy, grumpy, and utterly drained. But by day four, something shifts. My hunger fades, and I'm surprised by my ability to function normally. I even manage my mom tasks—making burgers and chocolate chip cookies for my family—without feeling the slightest temptation to eat. My willpower feels unshakable, and my senses awaken to a level of clarity I've never experienced. From the living room, I can smell a cinnamon raisin bagel sitting on the counter in the kitchen.

But then I make a critical mistake. On the evening of day six, feeling confident, I decide to do an infrared sauna session. That night, I wake up faint and disoriented, collapsing on my way to the bathroom. When I come to, I have no memory of the fast or how I got there. Scott is understandably alarmed and insists on taking me to the ER.

Lying on a gurney, I'm handed a small cup of vanilla pudding. Grateful for something to eat, I happily begin to devour it—until a memory rises slowly in my mind. I remember the fast, and what happened to land me in the hospital. Uh-oh. I freeze, spoon halfway to my mouth, realizing Lindsey's advice to go slow when reintroducing food was surely not meant to include preservative-laden pudding. With a mix of amusement and regret, I set it down.

Later, when I'm home, I realize that while the fasting and detox practices have helped clear toxins from my body, they haven't been able to touch a deeper grief that lingers, heavy and relentless. My chest carries the weight of something far greater than my own illness. Forests are burning, the planet is warming, and the world feels like it's spinning out of control. No matter how much I cleanse or heal, the existential questions remain, along with the deeper grief that feeds them—this ache of separation from something I can't even name.

Why am I even here? What is really going on?

The mold in my home feels symbolic—a microcosm of the larger decay I see in the world. It mirrors the destruction of the Earth, as if my body is grieving not just for itself but for everything we're losing. Traditional Chinese Medicine teaches that the lungs are the seat of grief, and I wonder if this explains the sadness I can't seem to shake—the mold illness somehow tied to my heartache for the forests and for the wild places we've damaged beyond recognition. It is as though the Earth's suffering has become my own, lodged in my chest with every breath. The destruction I've fought against for so long has seeped into me, as if my body can no longer bear the weight of it all

The late revered Buddhist monk Thich Nhat Hanh was known for his work with environmental activists, helping them overcome despair. In his teachings, he stressed the importance of cultivating inner peace as a solution to external crises. In an essay called *Environmental Interbeing*, he writes:

"Many people are aware of the world's suffering, and their hearts are filled with compassion. They know what needs to be done, and they engage in political, social, and environmental work to try to change things. But after a period of intense involvement, they become discouraged, because they lack the strength needed to sustain a life of action. Real strength is not in power, money, or weapons, but in deep, inner peace. The best way to take care of the environment is to take care of the environmentalist."

I would not be the first environmentalist to experience burnout from my decades of conservation work. I had read similar words many times before, and it seemed like one of those "nice ideas" that one considers for a few minutes, wistfully, before the reality of forests being strip-mined, air polluted wantonly, and children dying of poisoned streams and lakes sets in.

Yes, of course, deep inner peace would be nice, but there is an awful lot of evil out there in the world and I'd better get working. If not me, then who? So, while I appreciated and even agreed with the simplicity of his solution, my rational mind struggled with it. To focus on inner peace felt selfish and one that I simply didn't have time for.

And so, I had always pressed on. But now, I feel utterly lost. I can't possibly do more environmental work, and deep inside, I'm exhausted from trying so hard. My body and mind feel like a tangled mess, and fixing things on the outside is no longer the answer—it seems like rearranging the furniture when the house is burning down.

Instead, I decide to begin at the source—my own confused and anguished mind—and see what I discover. Thich Nhat Hanh's words echo in my head: "The way out is in." And so, "in" I go.

3
Down the Rabbit Hole

"Dive within oneself and obtain the Self-Pearl."
– Maharshi

When I decide to take the inner path, I don't know where to start. The last time I meditated, I was fourteen, sitting cross-legged on my bed in the dark, staring intently at a candle. I had read that meditation meant letting your thoughts pass by like cars on a train. Dutifully, I sat there, watching my thoughts come and go for what felt like thirty long minutes. Nothing seemed to happen.

"Is this it?" I wondered. "What is supposed to be happening now?" "Am I really meditating?"

Honestly, I didn't get it. I didn't see what the fuss is all about. I felt like I was missing something. With no teacher to guide me, it was hard to stay motivated. I tried candle-gazing meditation a handful of times and eventually gave up. Yet, even as I let go of the practice, my curiosity in meditation lingered over the years and kept me pondering about the apparently life-changing benefits of meditation.

Now, I'm 47 and ready to give meditation another try. This time, I'm determined to figure out what this ancient practice is all about. I've heard it described as a gateway to Shangri-La if you stick with it long enough—but in the back of my mind, I wonder if I will feel the same pointless sense as when I was fourteen.

At least now I'm older and (hopefully) wiser. I know I need guidance. A meditation community in northern Colorado, the Shambhala Mountain Center, offers weekend retreats for beginners, and I decide to sign up. A few weeks later, I set off on a Friday morning, excited for the solo five-hour road trip and hopeful that I'll finally find some peace and silence in my head.

When I arrive, I feel energized—excited to be a student at a real Buddhist meditation center. My bed is in a simple yet pleasant dormitory-style room, shared with eight other women in a beautiful, modern building nestled among the pines. After unpacking, I head to the dining commons for a vegetarian dinner with the group.

There are eight communal tables, and small groups are already gathered and eating. I fill my plate with veggies, lentils, and rice, then take a seat beside a few friendly-looking women—who, it turns out, aren't part of my retreat. It's a large center,

I soon learn, with many different programs happening simultaneously.

The next morning, I feel like an eager kindergartener on her first day of school. In the meditation hall, I settle onto a purple cushion near the front and listen intently as the teachers begin their instructions. Most of the other students are white, middle-aged men and women.

We are taught how to sit properly—cross-legged on the cushion with hands resting on our knees. The teacher explains to cast our gaze down at the floor about six feet in front (not closed, but not really open either) and to focus gently on the breath. If a thought arises, I am to simply return to focusing on the breath.

This all sounds simple enough. But the reality is that time drags excruciatingly slowly as I struggle to stay with the breath and allow my thoughts to pass. By the end of the day, I am utterly exhausted. My untrained and distracted mind is quite unprepared for the reality of sitting in silence for eight hours.

That evening, we gather in small groups with one of the meditation teachers to review how the first session went. The leader of our group is accompanied by an assistant, a young man who can't be more than 25. Curious, I ask him about his experience and learn that he has been at Shambhala for the past month, meditating each day, all day. "Really?" I say, in a tone that reveals both my incredulity and admiration. He shrugs and smiles. Clearly to him it's no big deal. After struggling with a single day of meditation, I sit in astonished reverence for his accomplishment.

A woman in our group is clearly upset. She expresses frustration with how little guidance we've been given, and I can't help but sympathize. I too feel like I've been thrust onto the front lines of battle with nothing but a pocketknife. I am not surprised, then, when I notice that she isn't in class the following morning.

Despite the challenge of day one, I plan to stick it out. I notice that the teachers have a distinct calm and grounded presence that I admire. One of them, in particular, strikes me as having what feels like "soft edges." During lunch, I tell him this, and the smile he returns has a knowingness to it, as though he understands something I don't. I realize I'm here because I want to know what he knows.

Day two goes much smoother, and although it's still quite challenging, by the end of the retreat, my mind feels settled and quiet in a way I have never quite experienced. I've been on long excursions into the wilderness that brought peace within, but this feels different—a peaceful mind suffused with a deeper level of inner calm and clarity. I leave Shambhala inspired to continue meditating and more confident that I have the skills to do so. For the first time, I glimpse the possibility of a quieter mind.

One of the teachers from Shambhala offers to guide my meditation practice following the retreat to help me stay motivated, and I decide to accept her offer. We have weekly phone calls, and it's not long before she encourages me to do longer meditations. I realize that for longer meditations I'll need a quieter place to meditate.

Our house is small, with few places to escape the noise of daily life with my young girls. After some thought, I decide to transform my closet into a meditation space. The first step is clearing out the clutter. I sort through piles of clothes, donating the scarves, trinkets, and high-heeled shoes I've only worn once. With the space emptied, I carefully align my purple cushion facing East, the best direction for meditation according to my teacher.

Beside my cushion I construct a small altar, arranging a candle, a picture of the Dalai Lama with his infectious grin, a few crystals, and a teeny-tiny Buddha statue whose origin I can't even remember. With everything in place, the space feels sacred. The ritual of creating this environment makes me feel like an official meditator.

Interior self, here I come.

I've been meditating regularly for a few weeks when I learn about a neurofeedback device called the Muse that monitors brainwaves in real-time during meditation and helps to focus the mind and keep it on track. Things are going well, but I can still use all the help I can get, and the scientist in me is fascinated by the idea of using technology to enhance meditation.

When the Muse arrives, I can't wait to try it. The next morning, I set the black headband across my forehead, put in my earbuds, close my eyes and follow the meditative guidance of the app, which instructs me to gently place my focus on the breath. Whenever my mind starts to chatter, I hear the sound of light rain. When I refocus, the rain softens and eventually stops. After my first session with Muse, I'm astonished by the power of this feedback. For me, the challenge with meditating is that I have little reference for what a quiet mind even feels like. As a beginning meditator, this device is like training wheels, letting me know when I've drifted off into thinking, and guiding me back gently to the breath.

After a month of daily practice with the Muse, I notice my mind feels less chaotic and more focused. While I haven't yet tackled my deeper despair, this progress encourages me to keep going.

I am using the Muse daily and have solicited the support of a neurofeedback coach, Dr. Cody Rall. During one of our conversations, he suggests I share my experiences in a Facebook group for Muse users. I start posting about the Muse meditations and brainwave graphs I've been generating with an app called Mind Monitor when I encounter meditation teacher and mystic Altair.

Altair seems to know far more about meditation and brainwaves than I do. He comments kindly on my posts, asking thoughtful questions about my practice. Our exchanges deepen over the following weeks, until we finally hop on a call. Altair shares his vision for a new meditation course called *Subtle Energy Meditation*, which he is launching with his colleague, Kevin Schoeninger. The course will be part of a growing community they call *Raising Our Vibration*, and he invites me to join.

I begin their 10-week meditation course, which catapults me even deeper into the world of meditation and the inner path. The group meets weekly and we learn techniques from a practice they call Subtle Energy Meditation. These meditations combine elements of Qigong, Kriya, Tibetan Buddhism, Hinduism, and Christian mysticism—all traditions that Kevin and Altair have studied for decades.

At the heart of these teachings is the recognition of a shared sentient awareness, often referred to as "no-self" or anatta in Buddhist terms. In other words, there isn't *my* consciousness or *your* consciousness—there is only one universal consciousness that we all share. This understanding is known as the nondual perspective in Tibetan and Hindu spiritual traditions, and it is accessed by inquiring into our relationship to self.

The quest to tame my mind has driven me inward to confront the most essential question a human can ask: Who am I? As I delve into this inquiry, I realize that my exploration of the nature of reality began much earlier than I thought—when I was just seven years old.

I have a vivid memory of driving with my mom through Pacific Palisades, California, passing by the Lake Shrine of the great yogi Paramahansa Yogananda. I was sitting in the car, pulling at the skin on my arm, and I turned to her and asked, "Mom, who am I?" I needed to know who I was beyond this physical body. I don't remember her answer, only the significance of asking the question.

The great Indian sage Ramana Maharshi taught that self-inquiry, through the question "Who am I?" leads to the realization of no-self. After spending ten years in an ashram, Maharshi emerged into the world in an enlightened state. In his teachings, he likened the question Who am I? to a burning stick that destroys all other thoughts—and is ultimately consumed in the fire of realization. In his seminal book, he wrote: "The thought 'Who am I?' will destroy all other thoughts, and like the stick used for stirring the burning pyre, it will itself in the end get destroyed. Then, there will arise Self-realization."

Looking back, I realize that my seven-year-old self stumbled upon this question quite naturally. And now at 47, I am finally confronting this question again and the other big questions a human can ask. I have *so many questions*. Questions like: "Who am I and why am I really here?" and "Is it possible to be happy in a world with so much suffering?"

I know there are volumes of sacred texts written about these questions, answers from countless wisdom teachers throughout history—not to mention the modern teachers of today. I've read so many books. And yet, no matter how much I read, the answers remain elusive. They are concepts I understand intellectually, but I still don't *know* who I am or how to be truly happy. My heart and mind feel like they're grasping desperately, trying to make sense of it all.

Slowly, I begin to realize that these two problems—Who am I? and How can I be happy in this world?—are not separate. They are one inextricably intertwined riddle.

If I understand who I am, the happiness will come.

Months tick by as I explore deeper into the recognition of self through the meditation practices with Kevin and Altair. One fall morning, I'm driving along Highway 287, crossing the vast expanse of sagebrush between Lander and Laramie on my way to a meeting at the University of Wyoming. Fences stretch along both sides of the road, the earthy green-gray of sagebrush blankets the landscape, and the peaks of Green Mountain rise in the distance.

As the melody of an Emmylou Harris tune fills the car, I find myself aware of the music—not just as music, but as sound itself. A thought arises: Is there someone listening to this song? I pause and sit with the question. Can I find her? I search for the "hearer," the one who is listening. Oddly, I can't seem to find her. It feels as though everything is just sound, happening on its own, with no listener. For a moment, the boundaries between myself and the world dissolve. It feels both strange and oddly liberating, as though I've stumbled upon a glimpse of the answer to my question, "Who am I?"

The feeling stays with me, lingering at the edges of my awareness. A week later, I'm still pondering it as I celebrate my 47th birthday. My daughter looks up at me and asks, "How does it feel to be a year older?" I pause. While I'm aware of course that my body has aged, whoever is here—whoever is aware of being asked this question—she hasn't aged at all. The same being that sang songs at Camp Tawonga is still here, unchanged. Millions of experiences have come and gone, but the one who is aware—the one looking out from this body—remains untouched.

Ramana Maharshi wrote: "The moment the ego-self dissolves, what remains is the infinite expanse of Being, untouched and eternal."

Through the months of exploration guided by Kevin, Altair, and the other teachers I've been studying, I finally gain confidence that I know what Maharshi was pointing to. It's a subtle but undeniable recognition of the unchanging essence of being that has always been here. Altair encourages me to stay with the inquiry, to keep exploring this recognition through practice. It's his guidance that leads to my next profound realization.

Later that week, I'm cozy in my meditation closet for another practice with Altair. I close my eyes and turn inward, guided by the familiar cadence of his lyrical New Zealand voice.

"Alright, we are going to begin this special practice with the understanding that every experience we have is new and fresh and awe-inspiring," he says. *"The awe-inspiring freshness in the vastness of non-dual awareness. Be totally comfortable and really check through your body. Ask it how it's doing and do that for a few moments. Find a way that you can be deeply relaxed and at peace. Unity consciousness means there is no separation between you and other. There is not two, there is just one."*

The meditation lasts over an hour. When I open my eyes and gaze around my closet, I feel clear, open, and spacious. There are no thoughts, just a sweet presence of being. Even the simple objects around me—the lamp, the jacket hanging nearby—look softer and more loving. It sounds silly to say that a jacket could appear "softer and more loving," and yet that's exactly how I feel. I also feel a glow in my heart, and somehow, the lamp reflects that glow. Then I realize something profound: I can't find a boundary between myself and the lamp. There aren't two things—the lamp and me. Instead, there's just one whole, inseparable experience. Everything is me.

The sense of unity feels like an all-encompassing wholeness, both inside and out. Yet even saying "inside and out" creates a boundary I don't feel. This wholeness isn't a concept or a thought—it's a direct knowing, much like the feeling of being in love. You don't think about being in love; you just *know* it. It's like that. I know this wholeness as surely as I know my love for my daughters. And because I feel whole within, the world outside feels whole, too. For the first time, the world feels inexplicably, beautifully complete.

Later in a text message I ask Altair about this experience, wondering if it's what "waking up" feels like. His response is affirming:

"We are all waking up. Waking up is about self-awareness. And no one can teach you to be self-aware. Existence is consciousness and is aware. Science and spirituality are meeting slowly on that point—a point masters and sages have been making for thousands of years.

In the evolution of consciousness, we are becoming aware of the world out there and the world in here. As that inner world grows, self-awareness grows. The true self offers us deeper, more conscious ways of living. And we, in turn, offer each other a consciousness tuned into creation—a consciousness that is relaxed, open, accepting, compassionate, and free.

We are finding out together if this path works. Not as a theory, but in practice, as direct experience, with the love of each other in our hearts to support that. This evolution of consciousness within us is immensely exciting and inspirational. It is supported by all manner of neuroscientists and physicists who are bringing the outer world and the inner invisible world closer.

We can be fully engaged in our everyday lives while plunging deeper into awakening. That awakening is unpredictable and deeply personal, as shown by our inner states and graphs. An open mind, free of expectations, and a deep love and support for each other's awakening is a path forged for us by masters for centuries. That is the path I am walking with you. One of great love."

His words resonate deeply. It feels as though all my life I had been watching an intense, dramatic movie with no way to exit when things got hard or scary. Then someone pointed out the screen upon which the movie was projected. Focus on the screen, not the drama playing out on it. The screen—the essence of your being—is always pure and still, no matter how intense the movie gets.

When my mind relaxes into that peaceful screen—into the true nature of my being—I access a space of timeless, boundless peace. I haven't developed the ability to reside in this expanse all or even most of the time—not yet—but I've developed the ability to pendulate between this peace of being and my small "Holly" identity.

And that shift feels monumental.

4
The Wound is Where the Light Enters

"Do not be dismayed by the brokenness of the world.
All things break. And all things can be mended.
Not with time, as they say, but with intention.
So go. Love intentionally, extravagantly,
unconditionally. The broken world
waits in darkness for the light that is you."

– L.R. Knost

I am becoming mildly obsessed with meditating (my daughters would likely drop the word "mildly"). Meditation has brought me real relief from the chaos of my mind. Amid the turmoil of my inner questions and the weight of the world's suffering, meditation becomes my anchor. It's a place where I can set the questions down, even if just for a moment, and find a glimpse of stillness. Each session is like dipping into a wellspring of calm, and the changes I feel keep me faithfully returning to my meditation practices each morning and evening for an hour or more.

The differences are undeniable—my mind feels quieter, clearer, and less turbulent. Given that just a short time ago I was plagued with an unruly mind with many intrusive thoughts, this shift is a miracle. And then incredibly I get an opportunity to scientifically prove it.

I've begun training to teach meditation through the NeuroMeditation Institute, founded by Dr. Jeffrey Tarrant, an expert in how meditation transforms the brain. When he offers a session to take detailed EEG scans of my brain during meditation, I eagerly agree.

When I arrive at his office, Jeff ushers me into a small, windowless room filled with computer equipment and biofeedback devices. I sit before a large computer screen, and he places a snug swim-cap-like device on my head with a bunch of wires coming out of the top. Finally all hooked up, he instructs me to begin my regular breath-focused meditation practice as the monitor begins to display my brainwaves.

The scans confirm both what I've seen on the four channel Muse headset (see figure 1 for an analysis of my personal Muse data) and the scientific research on the positive effects of meditating on the brain. After months of meditation practice, I have very high levels of alpha and theta brainwaves. I can't help but beam when Jeff declares at the end of our session: "You are the poster child of a quiet mind."

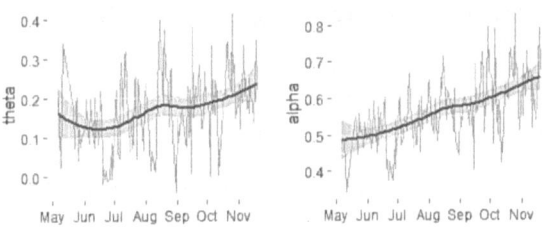

Figure 1

The scans validate my progress. My mind is quieter than I ever imagined possible. I even have data to prove it. And yet beneath the stillness, I feel the persistent ache of something unresolved—the weight of the world still pressing in on my heart.

Behind my house, the red rock trails amidst the juniper and sage become my sanctuary, my place to make sense of this unresolved tension. Here, I let my heart and mind wrestle with the unanswerable, imagining I'm Rey from *Star Wars* weaving through the rocks and trees, the trail my training ground.

My primary teacher and guide, Altair, is Yoda. We message daily, his guidance like a steady flame in the darkness. Running in nature becomes a sacred practice, a way to work out my questions—questions that have been simmering on the back burner of my life for years. I record audio diaries on my phone as I run, and share them with Altair as pleas for understanding.

Day and night, we exchange messages—his calm voice a beacon like Galadriel's light in *The Lord of the Rings*, shining in the darkness for Frodo "when all other lights go out." One morning I record this:

"It feels like another strange morning trying to find the beauty. Trying to find the beauty within. Why can I not see? Why does it feel so utterly elusive? Why do I feel so confused? I know the answer doesn't come from my thoughts, and yet I don't know. I feel trapped and imprisoned, made to play a play. When I look around and acknowledge that it's a play, that there's something so much greater 'closer than close,' it feels like a cruel joke. Because now that I know nothing external can solve this equation, the further I'm forced inward, the more I don't find it. The more confusing it becomes. It just feels far. That's the truth."

These words reflect a deeper paradox—the unspoken question of how to find beauty in a world so filled with suffering. Rumi's words rise up in my mind like a beacon: "Out beyond ideas of wrongdoing and rightdoing, there is a field: I will meet you there."

I've carried this quote with me since I was a teenager, but now it feels like both an invitation and a riddle. I long to meet Rumi in that field—to feel the unburdened beauty of a world beyond duality—but I just don't see it. I can't find it. With all that I've experienced working on behalf of the environment, accepting that a place beyond evil exists feels impossible.

I am constantly bombarded with stories of harm—elephants poached, whales tangled in nets, factory farms churning out endless suffering. Every news story seems to add to the weight in my heart. I find myself caught in an endless cycle of grief and outrage, unable to reconcile the seemingly endless horrors of the world.

Then, I read *The Book of Joy*, based on conversations between the Dalai Lama and Archbishop Desmond Tutu. One passage stops me in my tracks: "We are meant to live in joy," the Archbishop says. "This does not mean that life will be easy or painless. It means that we can turn our faces to the wind and accept that this is the storm we must pass through. We cannot succeed by denying what exists. The acceptance of reality is the only place from which change can begin."

His words feel like both an offering and a challenge. Joy, he says, doesn't come from ignoring the world's pain, nor does it come from fixing it all. It comes from accepting reality—not in a passive way, but as a foundation for meaningful action. But this feels perilous to me—like walking a razor's edge. How do I accept the world as it is without slipping into the treacherous waters of spiritual bypassing? How do I acknowledge the reality of injustice without becoming complacent?

I zigzag between moments of insight and waves of confusion like a ping-pong ball. There are days when glimpses of light pierce the darkness. Other days, like one glorious spring morning in Wyoming, I find myself utterly lost.

I'm on the trail again, reflecting on my life. At nearly fifty, I've checked all the proverbial boxes: loving husband (check), lovely house on a quiet rural road (check), healthy, wonderful children (check), dream job doing meaningful work (check)—and yet, given all these outer accomplishments, my inner space remained unfulfilled. *Something* is missing.

I hit record on my phone:

"I should be bursting with gratitude for where I live, for the life I have, for my beautiful children, for the beauty all around me. I should be bursting! There should be no container for the love I have. And that's what I don't understand. If this great infinite source and awareness is accessible all the time, why isn't it flowing? Why don't I feel it? I look into my dog's eyes, and he has it. He has that boundless gratitude and love. Right there. I've got to get that. I've got to find it."

Despite Altair's repeated guidance that the "it" I seek is "closer than close" and that I simply need to *feel*, I can't seem to grasp it. The simplicity he speaks of feels maddeningly out of reach. I am reminded of Luke Skywalker, frustrated and struggling to lift the starship from the swamp while Yoda gently insists: "Feel the Force. Life creates it, makes it grow. Its energy surrounds us and binds us. Luminous beings are we, not this crude matter." I feel like Luke, exasperated and determined. No matter what, I will raise that starship out of the swamp.

Renowned yogi Sri Nisargadatta's words offer a glimpse of a way forward: "The real world is beyond our thoughts and ideas; we see it through the net of our desires, divided into pleasure and pain, right and wrong. To see the universe as it is, you must step beyond the net. It is not hard to do so, for the net is full of holes."

But how do I step beyond the net when I feel so tangled in it? Every time I try, the weight of suffering pulls me back. I ponder: What if I were a great saint, capable of preventing 50% of the world's atrocities? Would I get to be happy then? Even under that scenario, the remaining 50% would still exist, and the pain would still find its way into my heart. How can I ever find joy in a world like this? Do we even deserve to feel joy in the face of such suffering?

These questions torment me, and I take them to the trail again and record:

"It's just hard being in this human body. I don't even know where all this fear and sadness is coming from. I really don't. It's just there. Really deep, old. Mine and not mine. It's this beautiful morning. So gorgeous and I just want more than anything to feel the joy and dissolve the self."

Knowing right from wrong, and tirelessly working on the side of the "right," was supposed to bring fulfillment. I've been down that road, and I've hit a dead end. For years, I've been what writer Bayo Akomolafe calls "slugging towards the looming horizons—the promised dwelling places for those who did not waver." I've spent my life following the so-called rules, believing that if I just worked hard enough, stayed on the "right" side, I'd find the magical land of fulfillment.

At 47, after decades of working in conservation, I've come to a painful realization. Rachel Carson, whose groundbreaking book *Silent Spring* catalyzed the environmental movement, has been a guiding light for me. Her work inspired my belief that more Rachel Carsons could save the world—if we just worked harder and smarter, we could fix it all.

But fifty years of conservation have not slowed the loss of habitat or the extinction of species. The pace of destruction has only accelerated. The harder we work, the further behind we fall. This belief has guided my own work at The Nature Conservancy. Every day, I believed I could make the world a better place by fighting back the jaws of development and the ills of humanity. This belief motivated me to sacrifice time with my family, to work long hours, to attend endless meetings and phone calls about which lands to protect and how to mitigate damage. Yet even as we celebrate protections and mitigations, the sense of futility grows.

The harder I push, the more futile it feels, as though I'm waging a war with no end. Rachel showed me the power of action, but what if action isn't enough? What if the change we need begins not with effort, but with a radical shift in how we see the world—a shift that begins with surrender?

This is where Rumi's field beyond wrongdoing and rightdoing haunts me. My work has been guided by the belief that if I just stay on the "right" side—if I work hard enough, smart enough—I'll find a way to make a difference. But what if being "right" isn't the answer?

I realize now that my struggle isn't just with the world's suffering—it's with the limits of my own efforts to stop it. The harder I push, the more I feel the futility of trying to "fix" what is broken. And yet, the alternative—accepting reality as it is—feels like surrendering to a tide I've spent my whole life resisting.

If harder and smarter isn't the answer, then what is?

I am utterly lost.

On my 48th birthday, I wake up with my face horribly swollen and a rash spreading down my chest. I feel impossibly defeated, exhausted, and wishing for the trauma of this mold to finally end. Cuddled on the couch under a fuzzy blanket with my morning coffee, I try desperately to find some solace. In my frustration and weariness, I text Altair. I explain my anguished, pitiful state, pouring out my misery. His response is brief and cryptic: "What are you resisting?"

I stare at Altair's words—*What are you resisting?*—and feel a tidal wave of frustration rising in me. Resisting? I want to scream. Yes, I'm resisting the pain, the mold, the futility of it all because it makes me feel awful. Isn't that what I'm supposed to do? Fight back, push through? But something in his question gnaws at me, quiet and insistent. I sit with it for hours, turning it over like a stone in my hands.

Suddenly from seemingly out of nowhere, an insight pierces through the veil: it's the resistance itself that keeps me trapped, like a bird battering its wings against a cage it cannot escape. The cage was never locked. All I had to do was stop fighting and walk through the open door. I grab my phone and type back: "This is about surrender, isn't it???" His reply is just one word: "Yes."

And there it is. I feel clearly for the first time that my struggle—the fight against mold, against suffering, against the way things are—has been my prison. My desperate need to end the pain has been the very thing keeping me trapped. In the moment of absolute exhaustion, at the bottom of the well, I feel Altair's outstretched hand pulling me up into the light of day.

"The wound is where the light enters," Rumi says. And so it is. God, I love Rumi. His words always arrive at the exact moment you need them. It's as though he has been standing on the far shore of a vast ocean, waiting patiently. I could see him before but had no idea how to cross the water to reach him.

As I fall backwards into the boat of surrender, I realize that the beauty I'd been searching for has always here beneath the layers of resistance and despair. A quiet, glimmering beauty, soft as sunlight on water, whispering that I didn't need to fight to find it. This realization lands so deeply that I seriously consider tattooing "surrender" on my arm so I'll never forget.

As Bayo Akomolafe writes: "Now the whole journey is the destination—and each point, each barren point, just as noble as the final dot. Every splotch of ink is become to me a fresco of wisdom, a beehive of honey, a lovely place—and every aching voice a heavenly choir. The world is no longer desolate and empty and exclusive; she is now a wispy spirit, whose fingers flirt through the wind—a million roads where only one once lay. And I need not be certain about the road traveled—since I arrived the self-same moment I set out."

The journey *is* the destination. I see that now.

The starship isn't fully out of the swamp yet, but it just wiggled. And in that wiggle, I feel it—a flicker of something ancient and unbroken. The beauty I've been searching for wasn't somewhere "out there;" it was here all along, waiting for me to stop fighting the world and simply let it in.

Joy arises not by solving the world's pain or erasing my own. It arises *within* the messy journey itself—the one that invites me to see light entering through every wound, every crack, every paradox, and every impossible question I've dared to hold.

5
Polishing the Heart Clean

*"We have the power to shift course.
It's our disconnectedness—and lost understanding
about the amazing capacities of nature—that's driving
a lot of our despair, and plants in particular are objects
of our abuse...Turning to the intelligence of
nature itself is the key."*

– Suzanne Simard

I'm on a plane headed to Costa Rica.

The kind stewardess comes down the aisle offering dinner, and I reluctantly accept. Gazing at the little plastic tray of chicken, potatoes, green beans, a teeny tiny salad, and roll, I contemplate just how much I'll be violating my "*dieta*" if I eat the meal. *Dieta* is the name for the pre-Ayahuasca diet I'm currently on, which prohibits dairy, gluten, fermented foods, and—most importantly—salt. Just how much salt is there in a typical airline meal? Probably a lot. I've been diligently avoiding these foods for the past two weeks. I already eat a gluten- and dairy-free diet, so this dieta isn't too hard—except for avoiding salt, which I've come to realize is in just about everything and makes a huge difference to the flavor of food.

I eat the salad (without dressing), vegetables, and a little chicken, passing on the rest and hoping this small divergence won't affect my upcoming ceremony. Content with some food in my belly, I put on my eye mask and do my best to get comfortable for the remainder of the flight, resting my head on a foam pillow wedged in the corner between the window and the seat.

In one of my very first meetings with Altair, he had said to me, "You are a shaman." At that moment, something clicked, as the truth of his words reverberated through my heart—not that I thought that I was suddenly a trained shaman. Of course not, but I understood the metaphorical meaning behind his words, and how shamans have played a revered and crucial role within indigenous cultures as healers and communicators with the natural and spirit worlds. I had this feeling that had I grown up in an indigenous culture, I would have naturally gravitated towards the healing arts and studied how to use sacred tools such as musical instruments, plant medicines, herbs, tinctures, and prayers to access these unseen realms.

When my friend Sarah mentions she has just been to Costa Rica on an Ayahuasca retreat, I lean in. "Really? Tell me more..." She describes her experience, and I'm utterly fascinated, peppering her with questions to glean all the fascinating details.

Up until this point, I had dabbled with psychedelics in high school and college, but after one bad marijuana trip, I mostly gave them up for twenty years. More recently, as edibles started cropping up and becoming available, I had begun experimenting with them at bluegrass festivals with friends, but never for the purposes of deeper healing work.

It's no secret that humans have a love affair with plants that alter our consciousness. There are many. In the Western world, we are most familiar with caffeine, alcohol, and marijuana. But we have likely been exploring these realms as long as we've existed, using them as tools for health and for transcending the ordinary mind. As author Michael Pollan reminds us, "For our species, I learned, plants and fungi with the power to radically alter consciousness have long and widely been used as tools for healing the mind, for facilitating rites of passage, and for serving as a medium for communication with supernatural realms, or spirit worlds."

Now, sparked by Altair's comment and a growing intuition about my shamanic leanings, Ayahuasca calls. The path of surrender has helped shift my day-to-day struggles immensely, and at the same time, I sense that she can help me release the decades of grief and sadness that have accumulated within my heart. So, I book myself on the week-long "The Nature Within" healing retreat. Now here I am, on a plane to Costa Rica to commune with Ayahuasca or, as my dear friend Kari puts it, "To go to the jungle and puke my guts out."

Ayahuasca (or Yagé as its called in Colombia) has been used for centuries by Amazonian indigenous cultures for medicinal, spiritual, and cultural purposes. It is actually two species blended together—the vine *Banisteriopsis caapi* (or Ayahuasca) and the leaf *Psychotria viridis* (or Chacruna). Together, these species work in harmony to produce profound psychotropic effects and healing. She is also known for her strong purging effects—she likes a clean house, so physical clearing is critical preparation.

A few weeks earlier, I had received a detailed email on how to prepare mentally and physically for the experience. The instructions included a long list of foods and other inputs (news, social media, etc.) to avoid in order to cleanse the body in preparation for the journey. So, I found myself in the kitchen boiling basil and rosemary in a large soup pot and funneling the contents into clean canning jars. Each morning before my shower, I would pour the herbal brew over my head, allowing it to dry on my body for a moment before toweling off. It was a small ritual of cleansing, aligning myself with the intention of the dieta.

As we tuck underneath the cloud layers and the plane nears the ground, dry brown grasses surrounded by the dark green foliage of the jungle emerge into view, outlining the airport. We touch down, and my body sighs with relief. I am here. Finally. I make my way through customs, noting the advertisements for posh resort vacations with happy families flying through the forest on zipline tours. My family far away in Wyoming, I wonder how many people in line are, like me, in an unknown country for the first time to experience a plant medicine journey.

The line isn't too long and in about fifteen minutes I emerge on the other side of the little customs booths. I pass through a set of double doors into the main terminal where the heaviness and heat of the Central American climate hits my body. Dorothy, we aren't in Kansas anymore. Exiting with a stream of other travelers, I'm confronted with a line of Costa Rican men holding cardboard signs with various names. I look eagerly for my own name on one of the signs but don't see it. A slight feeling of panic arises in my chest.

Continuing through the line and following the others outside, I spot another group of local men with cardboard signs. This time, I see the sign "Blue Spirit," the name of my retreat center, and my heart lightens. The man with the sign greets me with a big smile and ushers me carefully through the throngs of people to a van with a small crowd of women mingling beside it.

As we gather, I strike up casual conversations about where we flew in from and what we do to fill our time when not on plant medicine retreats. It feels like a strange liminal space—we are all here, waiting for something we can't quite imagine but have been called to experience. An hour later, when everyone has arrived, we hop into the white vans, finally heading off to the retreat center, about two hours west of the airport at the edge of the jungle along the Pacific coast. As we pull up to Blue Spirit, I'm pleasantly surprised to find a clean, Zen-like center perched at the top of a hill, surrounded by strange (to me) looking jungle plants. One tree has enormous spines around the trunk at least a foot long, protruding from every angle. The ecologist in me wonders, "What is that tree protecting itself from?"

Typical of my adventurous Wyomingite spirit, I'd convinced myself to forgo the fancy air-conditioned rooms and book a canvas tent, which is both the cheapest option and also located the farthest away from the lodge. It's quite a hike down many stairs and trails to my room, but the kind staff carries my bag.

Later that evening, following a delicious, organic, vegetarian dinner, we all gather in the large glass-walled meeting room in the main lodge. I enter to find a circle of about fifty cushions, some with people already settled in. I find an empty cushion and sit down, gazing around and taking in the energy of the other participants—a near-equal mix of mostly white middle-aged women and men. As the gathering opens, the leader, Eli, welcomes us and orients us to both the retreat center and what to expect in the coming week. We go around the circle with introductions, sharing our names and intentions for the week.

In preparation for our plant medicine journey with Ayahuasca, we will have two days for jungle steam baths, meetings with our shaman, Taita Juanito, and time for communing with the ocean and jungle. The next morning at the first light of day, I awaken to strange haunting screams echoing through the jungle. Howler monkeys, I think to myself, adjusting my pillow with a sweet smile on my lips. I drift in and out of sleep for the next few hours, then finally get up, put on a sundress, and head up to the lodge for breakfast. One of my favorite parts of being in the jungle is the simplicity of just wearing a single sundress. I would be completely happy with one great dress and nothing else for an entire month. Life simplified.

After breakfast, I head to the beach and spend most of the day in and out of the warm ocean waters, meditating, and lying in the sand. Tomorrow is our first ceremony, and I'm feeling that curious mix of anxiety and excitement to finally experience Ayahuasca for myself.

On ceremony day, we are instructed to arrive at 6:00 p.m. I show up just a few minutes before, only to find a long line of people already formed at the door to the retreat hall. *Apparently, they received a memo I didn't.* When I finally enter the dimly lit space, 36 reclining wooden cots are arranged in three rows, all facing the front of the room. The back row faces the others and is reserved for the shamans and their helpers, called guardians. By the time I find a spot, the prime locations near the front and back are taken, so I settle for a cot in the middle.

I begin setting up my space: a small altar with a picture of my daughters, a few crystals, and essential oils. The room hums with anticipation as everyone settles in. Time feels elastic as the shamans slowly arrive and prepare their spaces. Everything moves at an unhurried pace—calm, joyful, deliberate. A sweet energy fills the room as Taita Juanito and his guardians adorn themselves with beaded necklaces and feathered headdresses, their presence grounding and serene.

When Taita Juanito is finally ready, the lights are extinguished, and the ceremony begins. His deep, rhythmic chants fill the room as he blesses the dark brown medicine in glass jars. Flutes, harmonicas, and *chacapas*—South American leaf rattles—blend with his voice, mimicking the calls of the forest. Guardians move through the room, wafting the pungent smoke of copal resin from clay chalices. The sacred aroma permeates the space, clearing negative energy and heightening the sense of ritual.

When it's time for the medicine, the men in the front row are called up first, followed by the women. Then the second row, and finally, it's my turn. Kneeling before Taita Juanito and two guardians, I take the cup he offers. He blesses it, smiling calmly, and I press it to my heart before taking a sip. The taste is unlike anything I've ever encountered—thick, dark, bitter, with a texture like slimy mud. My throat rebels almost instantly, but I swallow hard, forcing the liquid down.

A guardian in a leather ceremonial dress offers me a sip of water to rinse my mouth. Gratefully, I take a sip, swishing the water around my mouth to gather the bitterness of Aya and spit it into the bucket she holds. Navigating carefully back to my cot, I lie down and wait. For the next hour or so, we lie silently in the dark, relaxing as the medicine winds its way into our bodies. The room is silent except for the occasional shuffling of bodies settling in. My mind scans my body for changes, wondering when I will feel it.

Then, from the front of the room, the lyrical notes of a harmonica break the silence, weaving through the darkness. The shamans are singing the sacred *Icaros*—ancient jungle medicine songs said to carry codes for healing and calling Ayahuasca forth. And call her forth it does.

The quiet is soon broken by the sound of someone vomiting. Then another. The chorus grows as, one by one, participants succumb to the medicine's purging effects. My own stomach begins to churn. Nausea rises, and I shift to my hands and knees, writhing like a snake to coax out what needs to go. When the wave comes, it's relentless. Over and over, my body releases bile and fluids from somewhere deep within, yet strangely, when I peer into the bucket, I see not its bottom but a vast abyss. It's as though my purging empties into infinite space. Finally, the wave subsides, and I collapse back onto my cot, exhausted but grateful.

Ordinary consciousness dissolves. The sense of "me" disappears, replaced by an expansive energy that feels connected to everything I've ever known or been. I exhale a soft "*om*," and my entire body vibrates from head to toe. Curious, I whisper the word "*love*." The vibration intensifies, humming through every cell. Each word that arises in my consciousness transforms into a full-body sensation.

I must be speaking too loudly, because a guardian gently shushes me. But I'm too far gone to care. I lie back, engulfed by the vibrations, disappearing into the resonance of the medicine.

And then, a knowing arises: *I must go outside.*

I rise and move very slowly, step by careful step, making my way through the hall and out onto the patio. A well-tended fire crackles in the darkness, surrounded by a few chairs. I sit, entranced by the glow, until another wave of nausea pulls me to the edge of the forest. Squatting, I offer myself back to the jungle. Each heave feels tied to self-doubt—doubts about the divine, about my own abilities, about whether I can trust the universe to guide me. Doubts born not just of this life, but many lifetimes. With each purge, I release another layer of doubt, until there's nothing left. I collapse onto the ground, emptied.

When I finally have the energy to rise, I return to the fire. Sitting quietly, I focus on the flames until a clear and gentle voice within says: *You are a keeper of the flame.*

The words crystallize something I have always known but couldn't articulate. My role is to hold the spark of light and joy for others, even when darkness seems to obscure it. As Altair once held the flame for me, I now understand it is my gift and mission to do the same for others.

When I go back inside, the shamans have begun individual healing sessions. Through the darkness, I can just make out the bare backs of men lined up, kneeling before the altar. I return to my cot, lying down and awaiting my turn. I must have fallen asleep because I'm surprised by a gentle tap on my shoulder and a soft whisper: "Holly, it's time for your healing."

I rise and make my way forward, joining a line of women kneeling beside one another. To my right, the shamans move down the line, one by one, their presence calm and steady. The woman next to me seems so strong, her energy radiating as she smiles at her shaman. Their connection feels warm and clear, like a current passing between them.

When the shaman reaches me, I rest my awareness in my heart, sinking into the comfort of his presence. His energy is cheerful, grounded, and kind. He asks in Spanish how I am. *How am I?* My mind scrambles to translate my exhaustion into words, but I can't find them. Instead, I motion with my body: depleted, weary, emptied. He seems to understand and begins brushing my bare body with a bundle of leaves—thistle-like, with small thorns at the ends.

He chants quietly as he sweeps the leaves over my back, chest, arms, and legs. The cool, rhythmic touch feels soothing, even as the thorns graze my skin. I've removed my shirt, and though I'm naked except for my underwear, I am too altered and exhausted to care. His presence feels protective, sacred. When he finishes brushing the leaves over my body, he slathers me with a cooling balm. Though I am still deeply tired, I feel strangely revived, as though some part of me has been replenished.

Later in the night, we are offered a second cup of medicine. When my turn comes, I kneel before the shaman again. He asks about my visions (none) and whether I've purged. *Yes, a lot*. He pours a cup of Yagé, blesses it, and hands it to me. As hard as the first cup was to swallow, this one is worse. My body resists, recoiling at the thought of ingesting the thick, dark elixir again. I drink it down quickly, forcing myself to keep it down even as my throat protests.

An assistant hands me a sip of water. I swish it around my mouth but don't swallow, spitting it into the bucket she offers. Grateful just to have made it back to my cot without vomiting, I lie down, pulling my blanket over me. *Here we go again*, I think as the familiar churning in my belly begins.

This time, it's not just nausea. A wave of grief washes over me—grief for the animals. It's not an idea or a thought but a visceral, overwhelming sensation. I feel the suffering of pigs, cows, and chickens in slaughterhouses. It's as though their pain is alive in me. One of the guardians hears my sobbing and comes over. I look into her eyes, desperate, and say, "I just don't understand. Why all the killing? It's not fair. It's not right. It doesn't make sense."

The words spill out between uncontrollable weeping sobs. The weight of it is unbearable. Even though I've been fasting and wonder how there can be anything left in me, my body begins purging again—waves of grief pouring into the bucket. Each heave feels like releasing lifetimes of sorrow. Finally, spent, I collapse onto my mat, tears still streaming.

When Eli calls for a third cup of medicine, a cacophony of voices rises within me: "Is this wise? Can I handle more?" But his words from the day before echo in my mind: "You are here for the medicine, so best to take what is offered." Reluctantly, I rise and kneel before the shaman again. This cup is the hardest yet. My body protests with every sip, but somehow, I get it down. Slowly, carefully, I return to my cot, relieved to have made the 20-foot journey without vomiting on the floor.

So much has already happened, and yet there is more. As I settle back on my mat, the medicine stirs within me. My awareness shifts to my chest. I take a deep breath—deeper than any I have ever taken before. It feels meticulous, as though every single alveolus in my lungs is expanding, infusing with life.

And then it happens. I am no longer just a body. I am a rainforest, my lungs the Earth's lungs, pumping oxygen into the atmosphere. The connections form like pieces of a puzzle snapping into place: breath, air, forest, grief, mold. I see it all—the way cutting down rainforests is choking humanity, cutting us off from the cleansing power of the Earth's lungs. The grief I've carried for the loss of forests is intertwined with the mold illness I've battled. It's as if I had to experience the absence of clean air to truly appreciate its gift.

Although it feels like it will never come, I look out of the large glass windows of our sanctuary space and notice the faintest glow of the jungle outside. Dawn. Thank God. Then, from the corner of the sanctuary, the most beautiful melodies I have ever heard start to flow from the musicians—songs of the power of medicine to cleanse the spirit—songs of love.

And then we dance, our bodies wrung out of all that would contaminate our ability to see and feel the truth of our greatness. Our hearts polished clean, in rapturous splendor, we unfurl our wings and dance for all of it—for the Earth, the Goddesses, the music, the jungle, the sunrise, the animals, and our collective human spirits.

Weeks later, I'm home and running behind my house, listening to a podcast featuring Suzanne Simard discussing her groundbreaking book, *Finding the Mother Tree*. She describes the vast underground mycorrhizal networks that connect forest ecosystems. And how at the heart of these networks are the older "mother trees," which care for and share nutrients with younger trees and those most in need of support. The system operates through reciprocity—giving and taking so that the entire forest can thrive. As Simard writes:

"Plants are attuned to one another's strengths and weaknesses, elegantly giving and taking to attain exquisite balance. There is grace in complexity, in actions cohering, in sum totals."

Our emerging scientific discoveries about plants caring for each other as sentient beings represent a wisdom once known and somehow forgotten—at least by Western society. It's as though when we shifted from tribal living embedded in nature to single-family homes, we suffered a kind of collective amnesia about the intelligence of plants. We took on a shared fear of nature. We vilified and burned the witches who knew otherwise. We got squeamish about spiders, snakes, and scat. We thought bears would come into our homes and eat us. We put God in a box to be taken out on Sundays. We sanitized our lives and put food and medicine in plastic containers. We disconnected from our deeply entangled and intimate relationship with nature, and forgot how the fungi, insects, and trees are here supporting the same life on Earth that allows us to thrive. We forgot that we aren't separate from nature. We are nature.

When I say, "We are nature," I don't mean it as a poetic statement or in purely material terms. I mean it in the most literal sense: we are inseparable from everything we perceive. The universe is one interconnected organism.

This is what the Sufi poet Rumi meant when he said: "Do not feel lonely, the entire universe is inside you. Stop acting so small. You are the universe in ecstatic motion." The Vedic tradition expressed a similar idea, suggesting that the energies of the solar system are mapped onto the human body. This is why, in the chakra system, each energy center is associated with a planet.

From ancient systems like astrology and the I Ching to modern interpretations such as Human Design and the Gene Keys, the same message is conveyed: the universe is holographic and fractal. From the frequencies in the human body to the planets, every single vibrational expression that we experience as "matter" is a microcosm of the macrocosm, with no beginning and no end.

I now realize that the Earth I spent decades working to protect had, in fact, come to my aid. In the moment of my greatest need, the Earth was there to help me through the wisdom of plants. Within the plants of the very forests my organization, The Nature Conservancy, sought to preserve, lie vital keys to humanity's quest to answer the greatest mysteries of all: *Who are we? Why are we here?*

As Simard says: "It's our disconnectedness—and lost understanding about the amazing capacities of nature—that's driving a lot of our despair. Turning to the intelligence of nature itself is the key." In what feels like humanity's final moment of anguished desperation, the forests are here to show us the way.

The indigenous tribes of Peru that I worked with call Ayahuasca and other sacred plant medicines "Master Plants." The Earth's Master Plants have brought me into a deeper intimacy and love for life than I thought possible, showing me that the Earth and I are one exquisite organism—and that if I want to care for her, I must begin by caring for myself. This means treating my body like a temple: beginning with nourishing it with clean organic food, speaking kind and encouraging words to myself and to others, and paying more attention in general to every relationship.

We are all related, and it all matters.

6
Becoming Coherent

> *"When the brain's electromagnetic waves and the rhythms of the heart are coherent, they influence and align with the electromagnetic fields of the Earth. It's a symphony of interconnected rhythms."*
>
> *– Rollin McCraty*

When we are born, our first beautiful breath announces our triumphant arrival into this world and we breathe 6-8 times a minute for the rest of our lives. Every inhale, we fill our bodies with the ingredients for sustaining life. Every exhale, we return the ingredients for plants to create our next life-sustaining breath. This reciprocal cycle ties our lives directly and inexorably to the Earth every single moment of our lives. What connection between life and the Earth could be more immediate or more visceral than our breath? If we cannot breathe, we die.

Human beings are the worst breathers in the animal kingdom, according to James Nestor in his ground-breaking book *Breath: The New Science of a Lost Art.* Americans are more stressed and depressed than ever, and one key reason could be that we have forgotten how to breathe. Nestor ties our epidemic of stress and anxiety to fast, rapid mouth breathing—and provides compelling evidence for us to return to a slow, measured and coherent breath of 5.5 seconds for each inhale and exhale. He says that "mammals with the lowest resting heart rate live the longest. And it's no coincidence that these are consistently the same mammals that breathe the slowest. The only way to retain a slow resting heart rate is with slow breaths. This is as true for baboons and bison as it is for blue whales and us." And so, it seems there is a critical connection between breath and nervous system regulation that warrants our attention.

The significance of breath goes far beyond the physical life-sustaining function in the body. Numerous spiritual practices use the breath to enter transcendental or higher states of awareness. One such practice was taught by Paramahansa Yogananda, a highly influential yogi who wrote *Autobiography of a Yogi* and brought Kriya Yoga to the West in the early 1900s. Profoundly affected by this book, Apple founder Steve Jobs famously gifted this book to every attendee at his memorial service in 2011.

As explained by Yogananda, "You cannot find God unless you can master the mortal breath. Breath ties the mind to the sense plane. As your breath becomes calm, your mind goes within." Kriya Yoga teaches practitioners special breathing patterns to awaken the *nadis*, or energy channels in the body that create the conditions for union/yoga with the divine.

The transcendent connection between the body and the breath is exactly the connection that researcher Stanislav Grof must have seen in the early 1970s. The story goes that when his psychedelic research lab was shut down through the governmental lockdown on psychedelics, he sought a new way to help people reach altered states of consciousness without plant medicines. He and his wife, Christina, started exploring breathing techniques and discovered that occasionally breathing fast and heavy can facilitate shifts that mirror altered states of consciousness such as those experienced with psychedelics. Their discoveries with breathwork led them to pioneer a method of breathwork they call "Holotropic Breathing" (literally translated as "moving towards wholeness" from Greek words *holo* (whole) and *trepos/trepein* (moving in the direction of) to teach people to access states of unity consciousness or wholeness through their breath.

We are collectively waking up to the power of breathwork as a nervous system regulator and doorway into the subconscious, allowing access to altered states of consciousness and releasing held emotional pain within the body. As explained by Nestor, "Breathing really fast and heavy on purpose flips the vagal response the other way, shoving us into a stressed state. It teaches us to consciously control it, to turn on heavy stress specifically so that we can turn it off and spend the rest of our days and nights relaxing and restoring, feeding and breeding." Nestor's book has been wildly popular, selling 3 million copies and a *New York Times* bestseller for 20 weeks—a testament to the renewed global interest in breathing.

As my interest in breathwork deepened, I became increasingly curious about other embodied practices that could challenge and strengthen the nervous system. There was something compelling about practices that teach the body to adapt to controlled stress, building resilience through intentional discomfort. I was finding myself drawn to primal ways of rewiring the body—practices rooted in the elemental forces that are so respected by indigenous wisdom keepers. Breath and cold—these weren't separate techniques but interconnected pathways back to our innate capacity for adaptation and resilience, each one teaching the body how to find coherence amidst chaos.

One Saturday, while hiking in the Tetons with my girlfriend Maia, she mentions her new daily practice of swimming for thirty or more minutes in the icy mountain-fed Gros Ventre River near her cozy yurt in Jackson Hole. She explains that she has been doing these cold swims and breathwork practices following someone named Wim Hof. "Do you know about him?" I shake my head.

Even though I know a lot of biohacking people, I haven't heard of him. It was in the early days when he was not very well known. Fascinated, I pepper her with questions as she shares some of the basic benefits of cold-water immersion, including how it increased something called "brown fat," or brown adipose tissue (BAT) that actually burns more calories than regular fat which stores energy.

Cold plunging, much like breathwork, taps into ancient wisdom for calming the nervous system and building resilience. In Finland, the tradition of *avantouinti*—a cold plunge into icy lakes after a hot sauna—is a cultural staple, practiced for generations to stimulate circulation, boost immunity, and sharpen mental clarity. Across the world, indigenous cultures have long embraced the power of cold-water immersion, whether as a ritual cleansing or a way to build strength and adaptability.

Cold magically brings us fully into the moment; our minds stop racing, our bodies reset, and something deeper settles within us. Regular cold exposure triggers a shift in the nervous system, reducing inflammation and flooding us with endorphins. As Wim Hof says, "Through the cold, you learn to reset your mind and become comfortable with discomfort, which strengthens both body and spirit." There's a primal edge to this practice that awakens something ancient inside, a grounded presence that, much like breathwork, invites us to meet life with a calm, steady pulse.

A few weekends later, I accept Maia's invitation to stay at her yurt and experience swimming with her. That afternoon, when I'm settled into my space for the night, I'm nervous and excited as we head out to the river. We walk a few hundred yards down a gravel road past several unpretentious Wyoming-style log homes and make our way down a steep rocky trail underneath the bridge to the river. The familiar and sweet sound of the snow-fed river tumbling and burbling through the rocks makes my heart sing.

We set our towels on a large granite boulder. I gingerly put my hand into the water to test it right before she dives headfirst into the icy river. Her daring bolsters my own confidence, and I head to a flatish rock where I lower myself into the water inch by painful inch until I am waist deep. And at last, I feel I'd better just get this over with. I dive forward into the freezing cold water. I start to swim out into the current, hollering and swearing. "Fuck, Maia, this is cold!" She giggles and swims around confidently in the middle of the river like an otter.

The river carries me downstream, but the current is slow enough that I maneuver to the side and the safety of some big rocks. It's excruciatingly cold, but I stay in the water, well past when I would normally get out. My skin starts to burn. Then suddenly and magically I feel curiously warm. I ask Maia about it, and she says that yes, this is normal. It's a "gift" of cold-water swimming. If you stay in long enough, the cells in the body adapt by closing to protect inner heat and you start to feel warm.

A core tenet of Wim Hof teachings is that our bodies have built-in adaptations to extreme conditions. Flexing environmental conditions through breath and cold—pushing the body to adapt—is what is so good for us. I can't believe it, but after about five minutes, I really don't mind the cold at all and am able to stay in for thirty full minutes, while Maia's dog Pippen watches us curiously from the rocks. When we get out, it takes a long time to warm up. The air is only about 60 degrees, but it feels deliciously warm and we lay together on the rock, warming our bodies in the sun.

The river swim experience ignites my interest about Wim Hof. Returning home, I google him and discover a wealth of resources on his unusual methods. In addition to cold water swims, Hof's approach includes breathwork practices with breath holds after exertion, like doing pushups. I experiment with his breath techniques—though the long holds are challenging and not quite my jam, his philosophy of pushing the body to adapt becomes a teaching that stays with me. This first taste of breathwork opens the door, sparking a curiosity I can't quite ignore.

A few years later, my curiosity leads me to an introductory breathwork session with Julia Mikk, trained by the renowned teacher Dan Brulé. Something about Julia's energy and presence draws me in, inspiring me to dive deeper. Within weeks, I've signed up for a year-long practitioner course to become a Breath of Love (now called the Solignment Institute) instructor, fully immersing myself in the world of somatic therapeutic breathwork.

We are mid-pandemic, so the sessions begin online. I don't know quite what to expect when I prepare for our first session, but I follow the instructions to get cozy: lying on my bed with a pillow under my knees, an eye mask covering my eyes, and a blanket draped over my body. My computer is beside me, its screen closed since I won't be watching anything, only following the audio guidance. As we begin, Mikk's calm presence and soothing voice guide us to take a few deep breaths. My mind begins to drift into the background as my body relaxes and settles into the practice.

About fifteen minutes in, a wave of tingling begins to spread through my body, from the tips of my fingers to the soles of my feet—a vibration I'd never felt before. I sink deeper into a state of consciousness where seemingly random memories and emotions surface. Earlier that day, on my way to the grocery store, I had passed a man standing at the center of an intersection with a cardboard sign, asking for money. I hadn't figured out a way to get over to him, so I continued on my way. But something about him stayed with me, and now, here he is again in my mind's eye, standing at that intersection.

Tears stream down my face—tears of guilt, sadness, and shame. How could I have so much while someone else stands in the middle of traffic pleading for a few dollars? In that moment, the image of this one man opens into something greater: he becomes a symbol for all who suffer scarcity and injustice. Empathy and compassion flood my body, revealing a deep, shared wound of scarcity and inequity. I silently vow that I will never again pass by a homeless person without giving something, even if it's just a dollar.

As I continue weekly breathwork sessions with Mikk, I notice that through activating and surrendering the breath, my brain shifts into the same slower theta brainwave states that I've been entering through meditation. In these slower states, deeply held patterns emerge, shining a flashlight into dark places—my hidden internal closet of unconscious beliefs and stories. Her breathwork techniques open a valve to allow these layers of pain and grief held within my body to finally release.

Convinced that breathwork heals the body in extraordinary ways, my scientific mind wants to understand the "how" behind the transformation. Breathwork feels like a portal into something profound, and I'm eager to explore what lies beyond. I've already gone down one deep rabbit hole in meditation, but I find myself diving into another—the intricate connection between breath and the body through the HeartMath Institute and their lead scientist, Dr. Rollin McCraty, whose extensive research links breath, heart rhythms, coherence, and consciousness in ways that feel both groundbreaking and deeply ancient.

Altair often said to me, "The heart is the portal." At the time, those words struck me as poetic, but now, paired with McCraty's research, they resonate as undeniable truth. HeartMath's work demonstrates how breathing intentionally "through the heart" in a method they call Heart Coherent Breathing creates powerful, harmonious rhythms in the body. But it doesn't stop there. These rhythms go beyond the physical body, aligning us with the greater order of nature itself. It feels like a cosmic key—unlocking not only inner harmony but also a profound connection to the universe and mystical truths.

According to McCraty, the physiological state of heart coherence attunes the body to the frequency of 0.1 Hz—a frequency that isn't just special, but sacred. This is the A-flat of the universe, the foundational frequency of Aum (Om) in Tibetan and Indian traditions. Mystical Kabbalah teachings refer to this same frequency as Aleph, the one "in the beginning." Even more astonishing, 0.1 Hz is the peak frequency generated by the Earth's magnetic field—and it's exactly the same peak frequency generated by humans in a state of heart coherence. Think about that: when we are in heart coherence, our bodies and the Earth are literally vibrating together at the same rhythm. This isn't metaphorical. Through intentional breathing, we're syncing ourselves not only with the Earth but with the fundamental frequency of the universe itself.

And yet, this connection goes even deeper. In 1952, German physicist Otto Schumann discovered that the Earth produces a constant electromagnetic frequency—7.83 Hz—now known as the Schumann Resonance. This frequency is created by lightning strikes in the Earth's ionosphere. As lightning discharges pulse through this atmospheric cavity, they generate standing electromagnetic waves that resonate at this 7.83 Hz and its harmonic multiples.

What's remarkable is that 7.83 Hz sits within the range of human brainwaves—particularly theta waves, which are associated with states of deep relaxation, meditation, and creativity. Though theta waves and heart coherence rhythms are distinct frequencies, they share a profound relationship. As McCraty explains, "When the brain's electromagnetic waves and the rhythms of the heart are coherent, they influence and align with the electromagnetic fields of the Earth. It's a symphony of interconnected rhythms." This means that when we achieve states of coherence, our physiological rhythms begin to resonate in harmony with the Earth's natural heartbeat, creating a profound sense of alignment and well-being.

This interplay between the Schumann Resonance and heart coherence is profound—different notes in the same cosmic symphony. While 0.1 Hz governs the heart's rhythms and its alignment with the Earth's magnetic field, 7.83 Hz synchronizes with the brain and nervous system, creating a nested resonance that harmonizes the body, mind, and planet. Together, these frequencies invite us into a greater state of wholeness, amplifying our connection to the Earth and to each other.

Inspired by this science, I decide to experiment with HeartMath's Inner Balance biofeedback device, a tool designed to help train the body into these coherent rhythms. This isn't some abstract metaphysical concept; it's measurable, tangible, and surprisingly simple. The device tracks coherence levels in real-time, guiding users toward the 0.1-Hz sweet spot where heart, body, and Earth align.

When I first unbox the Inner Balance device, I'm a little skeptical—it's so small and unassuming, just a little ear clip. That's it. I load the app, attach the clip to my ear, and follow the breathing guidance. A circle in the app's center shifts color and size based on my coherence level. At first, it stays stubbornly small and red—definitely not coherent. But as I slow my breathing and focus on a positive memory—the birth of my twins—the circle begins to expand, shifting from red to yellow and finally to green. My coherence doesn't hold steady in the green for very long, but even this brief success excites me. With nothing more than intentional breathing and a single positive thought, I can see and feel the physiological shift toward inner harmony.

I invite you to close your eyes and try some simple heart-coherent breathing by breathing slowly and deeply into the belly for five or so breaths.

Really do this now.

What do you notice?

It's so easy to overlook, but notice how in just one minute, the simple act of slow intentional breathing creates greater synchrony and harmony within you, attuning you to the natural rhythms of nature. And because you exist within an interconnected field of consciousness, by breathing this way, you add coherence into the greater field of intelligence that connects us all.

The astonishing truth is that the Earth is sending out coherent signals all the time, and your body is hardwired to move into coherence. The Earth's frequencies function like a planetary heartbeat, acting as a stabilizing force for all life. Studies show that this resonance helps synchronize biological rhythms, aligning the heart and brain's natural oscillations with the Earth's electromagnetic field.

Cold plunging and breathwork deepen this connection by acting as catalysts for resetting and optimizing the nervous system. Cold exposure has been shown to boost vagal tone and activate the parasympathetic nervous system, promoting resilience and coherence. Similarly, intentional breathwork tunes the body into coherence at both the physiological and energetic levels. Together, these practices entrain the human body to harmonize with the Earth's frequencies, fostering a profound state of internal and external alignment. From this perspective, interconnectedness isn't just poetic—it's biological, energetic, and deeply transformative.

Thinking back to that first icy plunge in the Gros Ventre River, it was about so much more than physical benefits. It was about discovering that our bodies are already wired to harmonize with the planet's electromagnetic field, to breathe in rhythm with the cosmos, to find our center even in the most challenging conditions—something humans have understood for millennia. Every conscious breath, every moment of intentional discomfort, every dive into ice-cold water is practice for something ancient and essential – learning to live as what we truly are: not separate beings struggling against nature, but conscious participants in the Earth's living intelligence, breathing and pulsing as one interconnected whole.

7
Attuning to the Vibrational Universe

"Future medicine will be the medicine of frequencies."
– Albert Einstein

I must look crazy standing beside my friend Emily waving my tuning fork in the air, believing that it might have some healing effect. Yet, that's exactly what I'm doing as a newly enrolled student in a training program for Biofield Tuning, a sound healing modality founded by Eileen McKusick. The method uses tuning forks to help clear and balance the body's energetic field. And as part of the course, I'm required to practice on friends and family, which is how I find myself here—beside Emily lying on a borrowed massage table. "What do you feel, Emily?" I ask, checking in as I hover the fork near her body. "I feel energy moving in my belly... and sadness," she replies.

I pause, tuning into my own body for clues about the shifting energies in her field. As strange as it sounds, the forks seem to act as both a clearing tool and a translator, revealing subtle information about past experiences stored in the field. McKusick often describes how the vibrations in the forks can "read" a person's history—grief from the loss of a loved one, tension from childhood trauma.

While I'm far from her level of precision, I notice something extraordinary. As I continue "combing" through Emily's field, encountering small pockets of resistance, I feel sadness rising in my own chest. Is it hers? Mine? Both? I gently guide the gathered energy back into her central channel—the core energetic pathway that runs through the body. "How are you doing now?" I ask. "Better," she says. "I feel lighter... freer." Her response confirms: this is not my imagination. Something real is happening.

As I practice on my friends, I'm continually surprised by what I feel and by their reactions. I had heard about chakras and auras before in my spiritual wanderings, but this invisible energy had never felt so *real*. It's also a reminder of how life leads us down unexpected paths that, in hindsight, feel perfectly aligned. For me, this journey began long before tuning forks. It began with my brother Mark.

When I was four years old, my brother was born with a debilitating illness, Tuberous Sclerosis. The doctors told my parents he wouldn't live past twelve. They were devastated. As Mark grew, his mental faculties were severely challenged, and he battled a variety of physical and psychological issues, including schizophrenia. And yet, almost miraculously, music became his refuge. Despite his struggles with basic life tasks, he took up the guitar and played with the ease of a savant. The tumors in his brain seemed to bypass his ability to create music, allowing him to play and sing with astonishing beauty.

For Mark, music was the hand of grace that pierced through the chaos of his mind and body, offering a way out of his pain. As he grew up, he learned to play at open mics and cafés around our California hometown. He celebrated his 48th birthday in 2024, outliving the doctors' predictions by decades. I believe that spending hours each day bathing in the resonant vibrations of his guitar was a huge factor in extending his life.

It wasn't just my brother who loved music. We all did. Many nights, I fell asleep to the sound of my father playing guitar and singing old American folk tunes. I probably knew who Woody Guthrie was long before any of my friends. When I was six, I started piano lessons, trekking faithfully each Saturday morning with my father to lessons with Mr. Bangs, who operated his studio from a small dark room just big enough for a piano in a little nondescript shopping center off the main street in Pacific Palisades.

I also had a love affair with musicals. On those long weekend afternoons when you're ten and time stretches endlessly, I'd pull out my favorite records—*Oliver*, *The Sound of Music*, *Annie*, or *Fiddler on the Roof*—and transform our living room into a stage. I became Maria spinning through Austrian hills or sweet Oliver begging for more gruel. These early connections planted music deep in my bones.

Then when my twin daughters turned four years old, I learned about a fiddle camp in Colorado. I had just started violin lessons with a local teacher, and as I perused their humble and somewhat dated website, something about this one stirred in my soul. I felt proud of surviving the previous four years changing diapers and juggling life with twin toddlers. A week away to myself deep diving into fiddle sounded like heaven. That evening, I booked my spot, eager for a week immersed in learning to play fiddle tunes.

Fiddle camp was pure magic. From morning until well after dinner, I was steeped in Irish, Scottish, and Bluegrass tunes, hopping from class to class. Evenings came alive with jams in every corner, followed by concerts and dances led by our incredibly talented teachers. The cafeteria food was horrendous—the other moms and I joked endlessly about it—but I couldn't have cared less. For eight consecutive years, I returned to Rocky Mountain Fiddle Camp, first alone and then with my daughters, where my love for Celtic music was born, sparking years of study and countless joyful jams, and nourishing lifelong friendships.

Looking back, these musical threads were interwoven so strongly into my life, that becoming a sound healer was inevitable once I went down the path of healing arts. I had already been exploring Reiki, a form of Japanese energy healing, when I happened upon a presentation by McKusick who had just released her new book *Electric Body, Electric Health*. Although it felt a little "out there" at first, her theory of the electric body and how sound and vibration could heal just made sense to me.

In her presentation, McKusick shared an alternative energetic view of the body and healing, contrasting sharply with the allopathic, biochemistry-based model of Western medicine I knew. She described how a person's energetic field—or biofield—stores a record of life experiences as vibrations, and that trauma and pain manifest as incoherence or "noise" within these vibratory patterns, like an out-of-tune violin disrupting a symphony. In her model, healing is the process of clearing this dissonance. Inspired by her presentation, I purchased my first set of 12 tuning forks and signed up for the next training to become a Biofield Tuning practitioner.

Weeks later, in class, I learn to "comb" through the biofield of my practice subjects—my willing friends and family—focusing alongside each energy center—chakra—of the body to detect resistance. Resistance manifests as changes in the tuning fork's pitch or tone. Initially skeptical, I doubt my ability to detect these subtleties. Yet, as I comb my fork near a fellow student's throat chakra, I sense a shift—a denser, "sticky" feeling, as though moving through honey instead of water. Following our training, I hold the tuning fork in this dense area with focused intention, and incredibly, the energetic "honey" transforms back into "water. After the session as we debrief, I ask her: "Did you feel when the energy released?" She confirms: "Yes, more energy started moving through my throat."

Once certified, I start integrating Biofield Tuning into my coaching practice. Most of my sessions are remote, so immediately, I'm working with clients around the world. What I experience is unexplainable by the materialist Newtonian science I grew up with. It's not supposed to be possible for me to feel the energy of someone non-locally, meaning not in the same location as me. And yet that is exactly what happens.

Although it initially feels strange standing beside an empty massage table with only a poster of the body to represent my client, I can't ignore what I feel. Every session reaffirms the phenomenon: I can feel the energy field of clients thousands of miles away, sensing and clearing areas of dissonance in their energy. Remarkably, these shifts often correlate with physical or emotional releases in the client. My clients consistently report energy shifts and physical releases, mirroring in-person outcomes.

Quantum physics recognizes the core principles of non-locality and entanglement, concepts that defy Newtonian science, and which physicist Henry Stapp called "the most profound discovery in all of science." Biofield tuning becomes my personal experience and validation of the quantum universe.

These experiences awaken my curiosity, compelling me to explore subtle energy at first within myself and then the surrounding environment. I develop a morning routine using the forks on and off my body for 20-30 minutes. As I pass the 174-Hz fork over my body, I listen for tonal changes. For example, the sound often sharpens between my eyes (the third eye) or mutes over my heart. Holding the fork steady, I focus on balancing the tone, gradually smoothing areas of resistance.

This daily practice sharpens my sensitivity. I use the forks to "tune" not just myself but also my environment—clearing energy in rooms and exploring the vibrational language of nature. I take them with me everywhere, including out in nature, and listen into my world—the trees, sagebrush, and deer—through the forks. Healthy trees emit distinct tones compared to diseased ones, and the forks reveal subtle shifts in spaces that feel "off."

Through tuning forks, the vibrational universe is coming alive, my body becoming a more finely tuned instrument, resonating with subtler energies and giving me valuable information about the world like a kind of "Spidey Sense."

As my body is waking up to the vibratory nature of reality, I see that for the past 40 years of my life, I have been living entirely within my head. My education and our societal norms had prioritized intellectual over intuitive intelligence, reinforcing a disconnection from this embodied wisdom. I had shut down my feeling body, and my conceptual, thinking-centered way of being was like a screen, shielding from view the subtle energies and mystical realms, and locking me into a very surficial way of being in the world.

Through careful listening, the forks strengthen my intuitive abilities, connecting me with guides and ancestors, and helping me to become more embodied. The forks rebuild the inner circuitry that decades of living in my head had disconnected. The forks begin to teach me a rich new language of vibration. I am attuning to an alive, intelligent, and subtle realm of the universe—whole dimensions I never knew existed.

I'm deep in the world of sound healing, Biofield Tuning, and frequency medicine, when a friend introduces me to a small but extraordinarily powerful device called Healy, developed by German quantum physicist Marcus Schmieke. Healy takes these vibrational principles into the realm of advanced technology, analyzing the human biofield and sending specific frequencies to harmonize it. The stories of practitioners and healers using Healy are so compelling, and its alignment with my work so clear, that I decide to purchase one.

What I discover is remarkable. Healy can access the unseen energetic layers of the human biofield—emotional, mental, and spiritual—and even identify deep-seated patterns tied to karmic or ancestral origins. It feels as though it can read my thoughts, tapping into the beliefs and fears I've been holding onto. Even more astonishingly, it sends frequencies to help clear them. Although the scientist in me was initially skeptical, months of working with Healy dissolve my doubts. I experience profound shifts: emotional and mental patterns I had carried for years—unworthiness, judgment, scarcity fears—begin to release, allowing me to feel more coherent and whole.

This coherence is not just personal; it is profoundly universal. The synchronization of the human energy field with the vibratory nature of planets is ancient knowledge. The I Ching, Kabbalah, Hermeticism, and astrology all reveal the same truth: we are embedded within a larger cosmic symphony. Each planet, asteroid, and celestial body emits a unique frequency based on its orbit. At the precise moment and location of your birth, the arrangement of these celestial bodies creates a distinctive vibrational blueprint—a kind of energetic fingerprint—that continues to influence your life as the planets shift and interact with your original design.

Among these traditions, Hermeticism offers a profound lens through which to understand this interconnectedness. Hermeticism, with its principle of *as above, so below*, suggests that the patterns of the heavens mirror those within us. The stars and planets are not distant, indifferent bodies; they are expressions of the same universal intelligence that vibrates through our bodies and minds. Just as the celestial spheres move in harmonic resonance, so too do the energies within us ebb and flow, guided by these cosmic rhythms.

Kabbalah deepens this understanding by describing the Tree of Life as a vibrational blueprint—a map of creation that reflects the structure of the universe and the human soul. Each Sephirah, or sphere, represents specific frequencies that influence not only the outer world but also the energetic patterns within us. When these frequencies align, they create a state of inner coherence, where the forces of expansion, contraction, and balance operate in harmony. This alignment amplifies our connection to the universal flow, allowing us to resonate with the greater whole. When we fall out of alignment, however, this dissonance ripples outward, shaping not only our own lives but also the collective energy field.

The I Ching, an ancient Chinese system of divination, provides yet another lens for understanding this connection. Its sixty-four hexagrams describe universal archetypes that represent the interplay of yin and yang—the fundamental polarities of existence. These forces are vibratory in nature, creating cycles of change and transformation. When we harmonize with these natural rhythms, we align with the greater cosmic order, allowing life to flow through us with grace. When we resist or act against these rhythms, the result is dissonance—both within ourselves and in the world around us.

These traditions converge on a single, profound truth: human beings are not separate from the cosmos. We are living expressions of its frequencies and patterns. Our bodies, emotions, and thoughts vibrate like instruments within a grand symphony, shaped by the harmonic resonance of the universe. Just as dissonance within an orchestra disrupts its beauty, so too does internal misalignment disrupt our connection to the greater whole. Conversely, when you cultivate inner coherence—when your thoughts, feelings, and actions vibrate in harmony with your soul's original blueprint—you contribute to the harmony of the universe itself.

This is not the metaphorical or handwavy metaphysics of the 1980s; it is vibrational and scientifically measurable. Your coherence IS the coherence of the universe. The frequencies you emit—through your emotions, intentions, and states of being—ripple outward, influencing the collective field in ways that are both subtle and profound.

Researchers at HeartMath, for instance, are studying the relationship between planetary well-being and Earth's resonance through the Global Coherence Monitoring System. Using ultrasensitive magnetic field detectors, they measure fluctuations in the Earth's geomagnetic field and its effects on global coherence. The findings are astonishing: changes in geomagnetic activity can influence human health, emotional states, and even societal behavior. Spikes in geomagnetic disturbances have been found to correlate with increased stress, depression, and even higher crime rates.

Just like the human body has energy lines or meridians, as described by Chinese acupuncture, the Earth also has invisible energy or ley lines, which are like guitar strings that vibrate and resonate within the Earth's magnetic field at different frequencies. Ancient cultures must have known this because many sacred sites around the Earth like the pyramids of Giza are located along these lines. It appears that we are swimming in a sea of Earth's electromagnetic fields that affects all aspects of our existence at far greater levels than we realize.

But it's not a one-way street. Just as the Earth's electromagnetic fields influence us, we, in turn, influence them. Personal coherence—achieved through practices that harmonize our thoughts, emotions, and actions—contributes to planetary coherence. Conversely, dissonance within us—anger, hate, or fear—ripples outward, affecting not only those around us but also the collective field.

The Global Consciousness Project, spearheaded by Dr. Roger Nelson at Princeton University, offers compelling evidence of this phenomenon. During moments of global unrest, such as wars or political upheavals, measurable dissonance arises in the collective field. Conversely, during times of widespread peace or unity, coherence increases. These findings suggest that our collective emotional and mental states directly shape the global energy field, reinforcing the profound interconnectedness between personal and planetary harmony.

Harvard-trained physicist Dr. John Hagelin extends this understanding connecting the architecture of the human body to the unified field of the universe. He says: "The amazing thing is that the human nervous system is hardwired, designed, engineered to reverberate in the structure of totality, in that structure of wholeness." He describes the human nervous system as a gateway to the fabric of wholeness—a structure designed to resonate with the underlying intelligence of the cosmos.

When the nervous system achieves a state of coherence, it hums in alignment with the unified field, allowing access to profound states of awareness—what spiritual traditions describe as Samadhi, enlightenment, or union with the divine. His science is nothing short of breathtaking: we are wired *from within* to connect with the divine. Coherence is a portal to God.

What these ancient teachings and modern discoveries converge upon is this: your personal vibrational field has a far greater impact on the world than you may realize. Physiological coherence—achieved through practices like conscious breathing, meditation, sound healing or working with technology—is the bridge from personal chaos to enlightenment, from planetary chaos to harmony.

To create peace within yourself and the world, you must first take responsibility for your vessel—every breath, every thought, every heartbeat—and guide yourself back to the frequencies of divine creation.

The Hermetics said it best: *as above, so below*. Indeed, it's all right there.

8

Love, Rewilded

"My work is loving the world."
– Mary Oliver

I'm standing barefoot with a towel tucked under my arm in line behind several other women preparing to enter my friends Bill and Joann's sweat lodge in the aspens behind their log home along the Popo Agie River at the edges of Lander. Voices are low as we chat a few encouraging words to each other in the chilly, fall Saturday morning.

Finally, it's my turn. I kick off my sandals, leave them neatly lined up beside the others and step forward in front of the small lodge opening. To my right, Bill guards the entrance. I feel his presence watching as I bow to each of the four directions, sending my heartfelt silent prayers for protection and gratitude into the ether. I pause and kneel on all fours and slowly enter through the low door.

The dome-shaped lodge is dark. Colorful Mexican blankets cover the dirt floor and hang from the willow branch ceiling. Warm heat rises from the glowing mound of rocks piled up in the sunken center, as I gingerly crawl to the women's side of the lodge careful to avoid accidentally tumbling towards the rocks. I prefer sitting close to the rocks and so I choose the first open space in front as my friend Annie follows and sits beside me. About six or seven women slide in behind us, their backs against the lodge wall.

It takes about 10 minutes, but finally, when all fifteen of us are seated and ready, Bill begins the water blessings, passing a wooden ladle carefully to each person one at a time. When the ladle is placed in my hands, the wood feels smooth and comforting. I gently offer a small amount of water to the dirt at the edge of the fire, then to the spirits above, and finally sip my own drink and bless myself, before handing the empty ladle back toward Bill.

When everyone has taken their turn and the water blessings are complete, Bill motions for the young man sitting at the door to close it. He grabs the thick cotton blanket above the door and lets it fall over the opening, adjusting it carefully until there isn't even the smallest pinhole of light.

It is completely, utterly pitch black. I hear Bill slide the heavy bucket of water towards himself and stir it with the ladle, finally taking a sip and then forcefully spraying water from his lips towards the rocks, sending hot steam into the air. He does this four times total, as the temperature in the lodge climbs. It's both stifling and exhilarating.

I feel my mind starting to protest saying "Wow... it's getting *very* hot," and then a voice of calm within countering: "You can do this Holly." I close my eyes and turn my gaze firmly within directing my body to relax and remember that I am fine. That I can do this.

Then Bill opens the circle for prayers. And pray we do. We pray for our mothers, fathers, sisters, and brothers, children and friends. We pray for the injured and ill. We pray for those who have crossed over. We pray for those afflicted by wars. We pray for the animals – the four-legged and winged ones. We pray for the trees.

When it is my turn, I pray for my daughters and my husband to forgive me.

Three years from when this all started... three years of ceremony, meditation, breathwork and sound healing... and I just did the hardest thing I've ever done. I ended the nearly thirty-year relationship with my husband, Scott. Although we were basically loving to each other, our relationship had been suffering for many years.

This beautiful man with whom I lived the dream of the Wyoming Adventure Life and birthed my daughters with, couldn't support me where I was going—and I couldn't go where he was going. We were not supporting each other in the ways that allow a relationship to thrive and flourish. Our human journeys were taking us down two decidedly different paths. My daughters were devastated.

More water on the rocks. More steam. I place a towel over my head. Even though it seems counterintuitive, the towel blocks the brunt of the heat so I can relax and let it in. I feel Bill to my left, motioning for the drum that I've been warming by the fire. I pass it carefully over and he begins to drum and sing a Shoshoni chant. I don't know what the words mean, but it doesn't matter. Like a mantra, the sounds carry a power and frequency that needs no understanding.

The pulse of the drum rattles through my body, the rhythm taking over automatically, as I sway front to back in synch with the beat. My body knows exactly how to do this. The combination of the heat, sound, and movement are wringing out the grief and guilt from my body, forcing my mind to relinquish the grip that has been holding so much tension. It's as though I have no choice but to surrender. In the suffocating heat, where I can barely breathe, I am stripped of all pretense and left with nothing but raw feeling. It is excruciating, and it is freeing.

As the steam rises and Bill's drumbeat pounds in the darkness, I feel the weight of my own heartbreak—the heartbreak of a marriage that could not survive, of daughters who are so angry with me, of a life that has unraveled despite my best efforts to hold it together.

And underneath all of it, I feel something even deeper: a sorrow for the Earth herself. My personal grief is inseparable from the grief I carry for the world—the forests being clear-cut, the rivers polluted, the animals disappearing. The drum seems to echo this grief, its rhythm aligning with the pulse of my breaking heart.

Finally, in the stillness after the drumbeat fades, a deeper knowing arises. A soft voice within me whispers: *This is not just grief. This is love.*

I lay in a heap on the blankets, barely able to move. The door finally opens, the glorious sunlight piercing the darkness as fresh fall air streams into the lodge. I crawl from the earthen hole utterly exhausted and limp, unimaginably grateful for the cool water that Bill hands to me as I exit and will help me prepare physically for the next round.

Four rounds in total, the ceremony takes about three hours, the heat of each round building, and getting even more difficult. The intensity of the heat only matched by the intensity of my grief—for the marriage that I couldn't make work, for my sorrow for the loss of my family, for disappointing my daughters.

And yet I know in my deepest heart that I have to tread forward in this new way. That to be authentic to what has birthed within me, I can't go back. The heat works its way into my body, burning the layers of grief, blame and guilt until there is only just me sobbing on the floor of the lodge, Annie's hand on my back for support, and the other women surrounding and holding space with their presence.

I had recently moved into a home that Bill and Joann had purchased for their daughter during Covid, renting space in an upstairs suite of the turn-of-the-century Victorian home a few blocks from downtown Lander. So angry with me about the divorce, my daughters preferred to live with their dad. It took a while before they would talk to me, and it was so awkward to have them visit at this strange new house. All I could do was to trust my inner knowing and bring love and patience to every interaction.

I am not quite sure where to start the repair, but breakfast seems as good as any. So, on Saturdays, I take my daughters to our favorite little café called Middle Fork. Over chai lattes, French toast, and Eggs Benedict we begin the slow process of repairing our relationship. Through the blessing of nourishing food, we talk again and lay the foundation for rebuilding trust. Certainly, I could have handled things better. This I know. And this I also know: throughout the heartache, pain, grief, at any given moment I had done the best I could. Every decision I made felt like the right one at the time. And so, knowing this, I forgive my husband, my daughters, and myself. Forgiveness is the balm that heals all wounds.

Through the sweat lodge, the breakfasts at Middle Fork, and the years of unraveling and rebuilding, I came to understand that mine was not a story of despair, but a story of love. I came to see that my grief for the Earth wasn't separate from my grief for myself. Forgiving myself wasn't separate from my forgiveness of the world. They were one and the same, threads of the same tapestry, different sides of the same coin, woven together by the Source of life that connects us all.

Ultimately, as Thich Nhat Hanh so brilliantly writes in his timeless poem "Call Me By My True Names," our joy and pain are one.

"Please call me by my true names,
so I can hear all my cries and my laughter at once,
so I can see that my joy and pain are one."

Our human journey isn't about erasing our pain. It's about allowing pain and grief to be a portal into the love that is always present. It's about holding space—precious space—for the grief. Not needing to make it better. Just sitting in the truth of what is and waiting patiently for the love that was hidden to be revealed.

In this sense, we are rewilding love itself.

Wild love is fierce and messy, tender and vast. It doesn't fix or tame or conquer. It flows in rhythms and pulses, in harmony with the frequencies of life. It burns in the fire, dances on the wind, flows with the water, and takes root in the soil. It holds us, not as we wish to be, but as we truly are. Requiring nothing.

And so, as I step out of the lodge and into the sunlight for the last time, limp and raw and grateful, I taste the exquisite beauty and joy of being alive. Love has come alive, rewilded, as though I'm tasting it for the first time.

And it is perfect.

9
Falling in Love with the World

"We sense that a more beautiful world is possible, even as the old world falls apart around us. Our hearts know it, and it hurts to live in a world that so often denies it. Yet this knowing is a seed, a promise of what could be. When we trust it, we begin to act from a different place—no longer from fear, but from love. And as more of us do this, we bring into being the more beautiful world our hearts know is possible."

— *Charles Eisenstein*

When I first set out to live my dream as a scientist, I carried this line from *Walden* by Thoreau as my companion and mantra: "I went to the woods because I wished to live deliberately and seek out the marrow of life, and not when I came to die, discover that I had not lived."

To me, living deliberately meant dedicating myself to solving the world's problems. I worked tirelessly as an ecologist, bringing my scientific mind to the task. I wrote papers, delivered speeches, and passionately believed that if people understood how special Earth is, they would naturally want to save it. It all felt so obvious. My conviction hung on the belief that at some point a collective "aha" moment in humanity—a shift in consciousness—was inevitable. But twenty-five years later, after countless hours of work, that "aha" seemed further away than ever.

In this race between consumerism and conservation, consumerism seemed to be winning. Centuries of Western science has given us incredible insights, but it has also trapped us in what Charles Eisenstein calls the story of separation—the illusion that we are separate from nature, from each other, and even from ourselves. All I could see was a planet full of humans disconnected, anxious, and trying to fix a world they no longer felt part of, as if we were outsiders looking in on something broken.

As Einstein once said, "You can't solve a problem at the level of consciousness that created it." My heart knew this truth, but my mind continued to believe it could find a way. Finally, when in desperation, I turned away from the world's brokenness and toward my own heart, the truth emerged. The world had appeared broken because I was heartbroken.

One night, deep in the jungle, I felt this shift come alive. During an Ayahuasca ceremony, I wandered outside under a blanket of stars, the sky sparkling and alive, and a melody of cricket song pulsing through the air—the Earth was singing in crickets. The universe was breathing, humming, and alive with presence. It was so utterly obvious that our lives play out as the Universe's grand chorus—each part a unique melody line, but all ultimately one exquisite symphony.

As Alan Watts said, "If you go off into a far, far forest and get very quiet, you'll come to understand that you are connected with everything." Indigenous communities have long lived from this understanding, honoring the living universe through prayers, chants, and ceremonies. Their reverence for Pachamama—the spirit of the Earth—is an affirmation of deep wisdom that everything is alive and connected.

Yet, Western society has dismissed this worldview, reducing indigenous wisdom to quaint superstition, while elevating control and separation as hallmarks of progress. This refusal to see our deep interconnectedness has left our hearts restless, longing for something we can't quite name. We sense that something is missing—but in the thick haze of modern life, we've forgotten how to find it.

It's the haze of modernity that leaves us perpetually wanting and longing with no actual answers for what truly ails us. No answers because modernity's solutions are transactional and distractions—buying something, traveling somewhere, experiencing something—rather than addressing the root cause of our suffering, which is knowing and loving who we truly are.

It's the haze of modernity that sold us on purchased happiness from a neat and ordered life with good food and wine, kids in good colleges, and a 401k, built on the staggering destruction of indigenous communities and ecosystems.

It's the haze of modernity that convinces us that more science and technology will save us, even though astounding technological achievements have failed to stem ever-rising biodiversity losses.

Don't get me wrong—I'm not saying we should feel guilty for wanting comfort. As I sit in an English pub by the fire writing this, I too am grateful for the ease and warmth of modern life. But here's the paradox: while there's nothing wrong with enjoying comfort, it becomes a problem when it numbs us to the deeper truths of who we are. The haze of modernity thrives on this numbness, keeping us disconnected from the wild, indigenous nature within us.

Each of these actions deepens our disconnection from the intimate, entangled bond we share with nature. We forget that we aren't separate from nature. We are nature.

What we've lost is the sacred understanding of interbeing—that nothing exists in isolation, and that every action, every thought, ripples through the fabric of life. When we forget this, we become numb to our impact and blind to the ways we belong to everything.

When I say "we are nature," I don't mean it as a poetic statement or in purely material terms. I mean it in the most literal sense: we are inseparable from everything we perceive. The universe is one interconnected organism.

When we retain a sense of inseparability, we feel a deep-rooted belonging and acceptance that cannot be undone. We love and accept ourselves, each other, and the Earth wholly, fully and completely.

Modernity thrives on our forgetting. When we remember, the jig is up. The systems that rely on our disconnection—the ones feeding off our numbness—lose their power.

This journey taught me to become wildly intimate with my own inner nature. Through this intimacy, I rediscovered the love and beauty that are my essence. I saw what has always been true: the world is already whole, beautiful, and made of love. I don't need to "fix" it. I can let go of desperately trying to repair everyone and everything.

The journey home beckons us to rewild our lost nature within. This is the nature that lured us as children to play in gardens, climb trees, and stomp in puddles. It's the nature we abandoned when we believed that having a house and a steady job would bring us happiness. It's the sacredness of all life we forgot when we put God in a box to be taken out on Sundays. The answer to our despair over humanity and the planet isn't found in a new type of green energy—it's found in reconnecting with the lost and forgotten parts of ourselves.

As my wailing cries echoed through the dark jungle, I pleaded to Source for animal and humanitarian justice. She plunged me into the deepest recesses of my broken heart where I exhausted every ounce of despair left inside me. There was nothing left to give her. And as dawn rose in the misty jungle with the sweet chirps of songbirds welcoming the new day, I came to understand that I am not meant to transcend this world into some better, other place. There *is* no better place. Earth is the most beautiful planet that has ever been, and any failure to see that is mine alone.

The path of transcendence and self-realization is not an escape—it is a grand homecoming and reclamation of belonging. It is a path of falling in love with yourself and the Earth again exactly as you are—and exactly as she is—not as you wish things would be.

In this extraordinary time, we are being called into a deeper intimacy with our humanness and relationship to all life—to see the beauty in what's here, the sacred woven through the ordinary. When we fall in love the world as it is, we awaken the power to heal it. And in that, we too are finally healed.

PART II
THE PATH AND PRACTICES OF INNER REWILDING

10

Maps and the Medicine Wheel of Inner Rewilding

"As you start to walk on the way, the way appears."
– Rumi

I love maps. As a conservation scientist, I spent years creating them—charting ecosystems, tracking wildlife corridors, mapping the intricate relationships between species and their environments. These maps didn't just organize information; they revealed patterns invisible to casual observation and provided clear pathways through complex terrain.

I've found the inner landscape invites this same systematic approach. In an era of spiritual overwhelm, where countless practices compete for attention and contradictory teachings create confusion rather than clarity, what's needed is a clear map. One that organizes the essential elements of transformation into a coherent, navigable system.

This is where Inner Rewilding comes in. Inner Rewilding is both a process and a map that unfolds like a medicine wheel, honoring the four directions and their corresponding elements that indigenous traditions have recognized for millennia. This isn't cultural appropriation but rather a recognition of universal patterns that emerge wherever humans seek wholeness. Each direction carries specific medicine essential to complete transformation, and together they form a systematic approach to reclaiming your wild, authentic nature.

The Four Directions of Inner Rewilding

East – Air: Awaken to Peace

The journey begins with the recognition of your true nature as awareness itself. Through the element of Air, you pierce through mental chaos to discover the peace that is your birthright. This establishes the foundation—without knowing who you are, all other spiritual work remains superficial.

South – Fire: Attune to the Living Universe

Here, through the element of Fire, you learn to sense and synchronize with the subtle energies that animate all existence. You discover that you are not separate from the universe but intimately connected to its rhythms, frequencies, and intelligence.

West – Water: Allow the Flow

The element of Water teaches surrender and trust. You learn to face your shadows, release resistance, and allow life's natural current to carry you. This is where you heal the crystallized past and open to the transformative power of flow.

North – Earth: Align to Your Wild Heart

Finally, through the element of Earth, you ground into your authentic self and step into inspired action. You shed what no longer serves and emerge as the protagonist of your own story, fully embodied and alive.

Living the Map: Returning to Your Wild Self

Unlike traditional maps that chart fixed geography, this medicine wheel is alive and dynamic. You don't follow it from A to B to C to D. Instead, you spiral through the directions repeatedly, each time going deeper, integrating more fully. Some days you may need the grounding of the North; other days, the inquiry of the East calls you home.

What makes this approach unique is its integration of ancient wisdom with modern understanding. Each direction incorporates insights from neuroscience, trauma research, and consciousness studies alongside timeless spiritual teachings. The practices aren't just feel-good exercises but scientifically-grounded methods for rewiring your nervous system and expanding your capacity for presence, love, and authentic expression.

To "rewild" means to return something to its natural, unconditioned state. Your wild nature isn't savage or uncontrolled—it's the authentic you beneath layers of conditioning, trauma, and social programming. It's your indigenous self—your original inhabitant—the one who knows how to live in harmony with both your inner rhythms and the rhythms of the Earth.

This wild self is not something you need to create or achieve. It's already here, waiting to be remembered. The medicine wheel simply provides the systematic approach to clear away what obscures it and to strengthen what supports its full expression.

The transformation this process offers isn't about perfection or permanent enlightenment. It's about developing the capacity to meet life from your essential nature—with presence instead of reactivity, trust instead of control, love instead of fear. It's about becoming so rooted in who you truly are that you can navigate any storm while maintaining your center.

As we journey through these four directions together, remember that the ultimate goal isn't to master the map but to become so intimate with your inner landscape that you can navigate by the compass of your heart. The practices and teachings are vehicles, not destinations. Use them fully, then let them dissolve into the natural wisdom they were designed to awaken.

11

Awaken to Peace

EAST – AIR

"Why do you stay in prison, when the door is so wide open? Move outside the tangle of fear-thinking. The entrance door to the sanctuary is inside you."

– Rumi

The path of Inner Rewilding begins in the East. East is home to the element of Air—open, spacious and clear. Air is the element of the mental plane and so it is here that you can pierce through the chaos of the thinking mind to reveal the awake, aware, and peaceful mind that is your natural state.

The moment you wake in the morning, there is a shift from the dream world to the waking world—a shift from unconscious to conscious experience. This moment, though small, mirrors the larger awakening that happens when you realize that you are more than just the thoughts you identify with. It's an invitation to experience life with fresh eyes, free of the filters that usually cloud your perception. You are invited to stop sleepwalking through your life and know who you truly are.

Ancient wisdom teachings consistently point to self-awareness as the heart of the human spiritual quest. The most essential question a human can ask is *Who am I?* This question is so central that over the door of the Oracle of Delphi in Greece—one of the most revered sacred sites in the world—inscribed in stone is the phrase, *Know Thyself*. The answer to this question is the truth upon which everything else must rest. As revered mystic Sri Nisagardatta said: "The root of all love is the understanding of yourself. You cannot love others until you know yourself."

Establish the highest truth first and let everything else unfold.

The Illusion of Separation

What blocks you from truly knowing yourself and accessing the transcendent peace of self-realization?

At the heart of mystical and spiritual traditions around the world, the illusion of duality appears again and again as the true source of human suffering. Simply stated, you are caught in duality when you experience life from the point of view as a separate "self"—a "me" that runs the show and creates a personal story.

For most people, this sense of self feels like a personal identity located somewhere in the upper body, often behind the eyes.

From the moment you are born, the experience of a separate identity is reinforced in Western cultures. You are given a name, taught to see yourself as separate—"you" *in here*, the world *out there*. Over time, you collect judgments, preferences, identities, and roles that solidify this sense of self. By the age of 9 or 10, you likely already have a clear sense of who you think you are: a person with likes, dislikes, skills, weaknesses, and a fixed narrative story of "your life."

As you grow older, your sense of a small "me" becomes more active, constantly managing, controlling, and reacting to life. You plan, analyze, judge, and evaluate, trying to navigate the world based on what is best for this sense of "me." It's the part of you that constantly compares, judges, or struggles to control situations. The more you identify with this voice, the more it shapes your experience, creating a sense of separateness from others until you are so blended that you have become this part.

The great mistake is the failure to see through the illusion of separation. This part of you that identifies as a separate "me" is like a character in a play. You have been playing that character so well that you have completely missed seeing that there is an actor playing this role. And to miss seeing this actor is to overlook the fact that underneath the character's thoughts, feelings, and dramas, the actor is perfectly whole and okay. As Pema Chodron says, "You are the sky. Everything else—it's just the weather."

Living from the perspective of the separate self is to live in *everyday mind*. But by shifting into what some teachers call "awake mind," or "Awareness," you tap into something much deeper. Loch Kelly, a modern teacher, refers to this as "Awake Awareness." Other traditions call it "no-self," "unity mind," or the "ground of being." It's like upgrading your operating system to a higher version of yourself.

The Tibetan teachings call this upgraded perspective shift taking a new "View." Buddhist master Mipham Rinpoche put it this way:

"When you rest in the natural state of your own mind, uncontrived and free from conceptual elaboration, you discover the naked, luminous awareness that has always been present.
This is the View, unchanging and beyond extremes—
Recognize it, and remain effortless in its expanse."

Where Do You Begin?

How then to shift into the View? Start with a simple question: *Are you aware?*

When you ask yourself this, something profound happens. You pause. You check in with yourself. And in that moment of knowing that you *are* aware, you begin to glimpse your true nature. Something had to answer the question. You—Awareness—know you are aware. Therefore, you are not your thoughts. You are the Awareness in which thoughts arise. You are the space in which everything, including thinking appears.

Now, ask yourself: What can you say about Awareness—about *you*?

Objects—like your thoughts, feelings, and perceptions—have boundaries. Do you, Awareness, have boundaries? Objects come and go in time. Do you, Awareness, come and go in time?

As you shift your perspective, you begin to realize that everything you experience—what you see, hear, taste, touch, and even think—is an object appearing in Awareness. But you are not an object. You are the subject—you are Awareness in which everything appears. It's like realizing you are not bound to the chaotic scene in a movie, but the pristine screen upon which the movie plays. As modern spiritual teacher Mooji says: "To live as an object is ignorance. To live as the subject is freedom and natural joy."

Consciousness at the Heart of Awakening

It may seem too simple—too obvious—that by turning your attention from the objects of your experience toward the awareness that perceives them, you reconnect with your true nature. But the Buddha, when he emerged from under the Bodhi tree after his enlightenment, said that if he were to tell others the truth, they wouldn't believe him because it is *so simple.*

Consciousness is not something you can grasp with the intellect or thinking mind.

Close your eyes for a moment. In the stillness space, beyond thinking, what is here? It's so simple, ordinary and obvious that it's easy to overlook. You are aware. Awareness is here. Awareness is present even when you're not thinking, even when there's no specific object of attention. That is your true nature. It's not located in your body, and it's not limited by time or space. It simply *is*—infinite and ever-present.

When you shift into the view as Awareness, you become aware that you are, in fact, consciousness itself. As physicist Max

Planck famously said: "I regard consciousness as fundamental. I regard matter as derivative from consciousness."

Modern physicist Donald Hoffman says that the material world and spacetime are not primary realities; they emerge from a deeper consciousness. This understanding marks the next great leap in human evolution—the realization that consciousness, not matter, is primary. Einstein himself appears to have understood this as well, saying, "The greatest illusion in the world is the illusion of separation." What we call "matter" is actually made of consciousness.

The Freedom You Seek

The freedom you seek is right here, in Awareness. Let go of your identification with a separate personhood. Release any ideas you have about yourself. Let go of thinking. Journey the ten inches from the chaos of the thinking mind to the peaceful space of the heart. Be the calm within the storm. Be the "not-knowing" that knows.

I hear you asking: Is this it? Is this enlightenment? And the answer is a resounding yes and no. Yes, because to be "enlightened" is to awaken to the peace of being. It isn't something you have to get to achieve like a video game where you jump through enough hoops to get to the next level. Life is not a video game. The end is always right at the beginning where you start. At the same time, life is an unfolding process of becoming. There is no destination. There is simply an ever-present unfolding beginning and ending all the time.

To participate awake in the world is our great journey. It is our joy and what we signed up for.

...

Essential Practices

Sacred Daily Meditation Practice

I cannot emphasize more strongly how important a daily practice has been in my journey. My daily practice is my foundation, anchoring and setting the energy for the day. I invite you to personalize it as your own sacred practice—one that feels nourishing, grounding, and aligned with your heart.

Step 1: Establish a Sacred Space for Your Practice

It is essential to have a dedicated space for your inner journey. This does not need to be elaborate or large—just a space that feels intentional and supportive. My first meditation space was a walk-in closet, simply because I lived in a home where every bedroom was occupied, and there wasn't another room available for meditation. It wasn't fancy, but it worked. What matters most is having a special place for your practice, a space that signals to your body and mind that this is time for stillness, reflection, and connection.

Step 2: Create a Personal Altar

An altar serves as an energetic anchor for your practice. I love my altar so much—it is a living expression of my connection to the sacred. Altars have been used for centuries across spiritual traditions because they create a focal point for devotion and inner connection. I have both a private meditation altar and one in my living room, each serving as a visible reminder of the sacred in my life.

To begin, place a cloth as the base of your altar—this could be as simple as a white cloth napkin or a colorful fabric that you love. Then, add objects that inspire you: stones, feathers, flowers, candles, or images that connect you to wild places. Let your altar be a reflection of your heart. By tending to this space with intention, you cultivate a sacred connection to the Earth and to your practice, a quiet reminder of the reciprocity that sustains all life.

Step 3: Discovering Awareness Practices

You cannot think your way into discovering your true nature. Awareness is not something to be grasped—it is something to be recognized. The practices below are modern interpretations of ancient Tibetan teachings like Dzogchen and Mahamudra, which use short meditations, called "pith instructions," to point directly to the truth of who you are.

As you prepare for these practices, take a few moments to ground yourself. Sit comfortably with your back straight, your feet flat on the floor, and your hands resting gently in your lap. Close your eyes, take a long, slow, deep breath, and simply be present with what is here now. There is nothing to fix, nothing to change. Just rest in the awareness of this moment, and allow yourself to explore the depth of your own being.

...

Awareness Practice 1: Are You Aware?
Ask yourself: *Are you aware?*

Pause, notice, and check who or what answers this question.

Awareness Practice 2:
No One is Listening. No One is Seeing.
Ask yourself: *Who is hearing? Where is the hearer? Who is seeing? Where is the seer?*

Inquire and notice if you can find the one who is hearing or seeing in your experience right now.

Pause, notice, and check if you can find a "you" as the hearer or seer.

Notice that in Awareness, there is no separate one listening or seeing.

Awareness Practice 3: Return to Awareness
Guided meditation available on inner-rewilding.com

Awareness Practice 4: Lion's Gaze
Find a place with a wide view—where the landscape and sky stretch out before you. Or, if that isn't available, even a large room will suffice. Allow your gaze to soften, so that you are no longer focused on anything in particular. Then, bring this openness into your mind. Let there be no distinction between the space around you and the space inside. As you hold this view, notice the seamless field of being, where the "me" drops away.

Awareness Practice 5: You Are Everywhere.
This is best done with a partner.

Sit in front of them and close your eyes.

Ask: *Can you find a place in your experience where they end and you begin?*

Notice that in Awareness there is no place where you end and they begin.

Awareness Practice 6: There is Nothing to Know.

In today's world, it's easy to get caught in an endless cycle of gathering information, as if knowledge will somehow lead us to happiness. We accumulate facts, ideas, and data, believing that once we have enough, we'll "get there"—to that place of fulfillment and enlightenment. But this pattern only keeps us seeking happiness outside ourselves.

The key, however, is to let go of the need to know. What if there is nothing more you need to know to find peace?

12

Attune to the Living Universe

SOUTH – FIRE

"Each celestial body, in fact each and every atom, produces a particular sound on account of its movement, its rhythm or vibration. All these sounds and vibrations form a universal harmony in which each element, while having its own function and character, contributes to the whole."

– *Pythagoras (569-475 BC)*

I once believed I was deeply attuned to the natural world. As a scientist, I spent years studying its rhythms, measuring its patterns, and documenting its wonders. Nature was my life's work, my daily devotion. Yet, in hindsight, I can see that I wasn't truly attuned. I knew nature as an observer, but I didn't *feel* nature inside as part of me.

I discovered that attuning to the living universe isn't about observing it—it's about sensing and embodying it at the level of subtle energy and beyond. This wasn't something I could have predicted, analyzed, or charted on a graph, or even understood with the analytical mind. And yet, I cannot deny the profound transformation that unfolded when I began to attune to the subtle energies and frequencies of life.

In the Inner Rewilding path, South represents the energies of the living universe alive within everything through the element of Fire. The animate worldview is held by indigenous cultures around the world, including a Peruvian shaman I've studied with. Sitting in Zoom meetings with him, he would frequently remark on something happening outside: Sudden rain? That's a message. A hawk flying overhead? That's a message. Pipe smoke drifting to the left? That's a message.

From this perspective, literally *everything* carries a potential message because the universe is alive and speaking to you all the time through everything happening around you. With this view comes an implicit understanding that everything is consciousness. There's no "dead" substance in the universe called matter, separate from consciousness.

This perspective might seem quaint or nonsensical through the lens of modern, scientific materialism. But the truth is that animism has been the predominant worldview of indigenous cultures for millennia, and Western culture is awakening to the profound wisdom they have preserved. People are turning to the teachings of those who have not lost their connections to the living universe.

It makes sense, doesn't it? When humans live in close contact with the Earth, our senses stay sharp, our perception keen.

Indigenous wisdom invites us to become more sensitive, more embodied, and more attuned to these subtle energies. Growing up in the natural world fosters an intimate embodied connection to it and a knowing that plants, animals, rivers, mountains, and even weather patterns are imbued with spirit or consciousness. With the help of consciousness-expanding plants like mushrooms, San Pedro, or Ayahuasca, which have been used by indigenous people for millennia, this becomes obvious.

Yet, this understanding isn't confined to ancient cultures or shamanic practices. It's mirrored in cosmological insights and spiritual traditions from around the world. At their core, they share a profound recognition of vibration as the foundation of all existence—a universal rhythm that connects every particle, every being, every breath.

This contrasts sharply with the cosmological story of the Big Bang that I was taught in my high school physics class—the extraordinary moment in time when our known universe burst forth from an infinitesimally small particle into being. Devoid of context, this explanation has a "so what" feeling to me, like explaining what notes are in music without hearing the symphony.

The Big Breath

Ancient Vedic teachings speak of the universe's first expression as a primordial vibration—the sacred sound of *Aum* or *Om*. Leading cosmologists like Dr. Jude Currivan reimagine the moment of creation not as a chaotic big bang, but as a "big breath." She writes:

"Beginning 13.8 billion years ago not in the implied chaos of the big bang but as the first moment of a wonderfully fine-tuned, beautifully ordered and ongoing big breath, our unified conscious and essentially living universe exists to evolve."

From this "big breath," a sea of coherent vibration emerged—a universal rhythm of life force energy. This vibratory essence, known as *Shakti* in Hindu theology (or *Qi, Prana, Lung,* or *Mana* in other traditions), flows through every aspect of existence and emerges from *Shiva*—pure consciousness.

For millennia, shamans, mystics, and indigenous wisdom keepers have supported people to attune to this vibratory essence through ceremony, drumming, dance, and communion with nature. These practices helped humans come into rhythm with the naturally healing frequencies of the Earth. In contrast, because our Western understanding did not acknowledge this vibratory essence at the foundation of existence, we ignored and disconnected from the nature-based wisdom and practices that had long supported human well-being.

Despite modern education that instilled a "dead" universe story in our heads, a deeper knowing persists. We know that nature is healing and good for us. We know that we feel better when we walk in a forest or breathe fresh ocean air. It's undeniable.

We intrinsically know this healing power of nature, yet it can feel difficult to sense the living force within all matter because we have created a world filled with incoherent energies like wifi, cell towers, buildings, cars, fluorescent lighting, and machinery noise that jam this clear coherent signal.

How do you begin to attune yourself to this living universe within?

The Sacred Technology of Breath

Indigenous cultures and wisdom traditions have long utilized rhythmic drumming, chanting, and mantra to synchronize humans to the vibratory pulse of the universe and create portals to internal coherence. However, the simplest and most natural practice is to begin with the breath. The breath is our built-in technology to reestablish physiological coherence through what's called your resonant frequency—your personal frequency of coherence.

When you breathe deeply and slowly at 5 to 7 breaths per minute in heart coherence, you are attuning to the ideal frequency for human physiology, 0.1 Hz. This breath cycle creates a resonance between the heart and nervous system, which in turn can support deeper states of awareness, relaxation, and connection with nature.

As research from HeartMath shows, cultivating heart coherence not only harmonizes the body but also transforms how you perceive and interact with the world:

"When we are in heart coherence, our physical, emotional, and mental systems align, creating a state of harmony and flow. In this state, we're better able to access intuition, respond to challenges with resilience, and experience a deeper connection to ourselves and the world around us."

By practicing heart-coherent breathing, you bring your body into alignment with a universal rhythm—one that fosters emotional balance and physiological health. This creates an internal harmony that, over time, may also synchronize with the Earth's larger electromagnetic field, fostering an expanded sense of connection.

This breath practice literally synchronizes you with the vibratory intelligence of the cosmos, creating the conditions for personal healing and global harmony. The Fire element is a purifier, a force of transformation, enabling you to release chaotic patterns and attune to the living universe's rhythm.

Through the breath also lies the deeper activation of the body's energy system, rooted in the central channel described in Vedic traditions as the *sushumna nadi*. This energetic pathway runs from the base of the spine to the crown of the head, connecting the seven energy chakras—the vibratory centers that harmonize our inner and outer worlds.

Central Channel Breathing is a transformative practice that awakens this flow of life force energy. By visualizing the breath traveling up and down this central channel, you activate the sacred *Shakti* fire—the kundalini energy—at the base of the spine and invite these portals of energy to open.

I'll be honest. When I began these practices for the first time, I didn't feel much. But through daily practice, I grooved the channels of energy within my body, waking them up. After a few weeks of practice, I could feel a subtle flow of energy and tingling at the top of my head. I found that this practice required both faith and patience to keep going, knowing that something was happening even if I couldn't feel it yet.

Attuning Through Frequency

Waking up the body through breath practices is essential somatic work. However, as Nikola Tesla said, "If you want to know the secrets of the universe, think energy, frequency and vibration." Whether through natural modalities like tuning forks, mantra, and crystal bowls or emerging technologies, working with frequency is a powerful way to bring your body and mind into harmony with the Earth and the cosmos.

I first began working with tuning forks. Tuning forks emit precise frequencies that resonate with the natural vibrations of the universe, much like a musical instrument being tuned, and I became fascinated by the way that the universe would communicate to me through the forks. I learned to "read" the energetic universe like a book through the forks. Frequency-based technologies are also available that use light and sound to catalyze healing processes within your body and the surrounding biofield.

These tools invite you to consider your body's health and well-being through the lens of the vibratory universe and harness your body's natural ability to heal through frequency. They don't just bring balance; they expand your awareness of the vibratory language all around you—the pull of the tides, the rhythm of the moon, and the pulse of your own heartbeat. They remind you that attuning to the living universe is not just about external observation but about reconnecting to the sacred conversation of life happening through the frequencies within and all around you.

Working with Sacred Plant Allies

Throughout history, sacred Master Plants have been revered as powerful allies for deepening our connection to nature, ourselves, and the vast web of life. One such plant that has played a special role in my own journey is Ayahuasca. Ayahuasca, brewed from the Banisteriopsis caapi vine and Chacruna, has been used by indigenous tribes in the Amazon for centuries as a tool for healing and spiritual insight. Often referred to as the "vine of the soul," Ayahuasca opens the door to profound transformation by dissolving illusions of separateness and reconnecting you with the greater whole.

When taken in ceremonial settings under the guidance of experienced shamans (a crucial distinction), Ayahuasca has the power to illuminate deep truths, clear emotional blockages, and awaken you to the interconnectedness of all life. Her lessons can be challenging, requiring humility, courage, and surrender. She is definitely not for everyone. Yet, if you feel called to meet her, she offers extraordinary opportunities for growth, healing, and connection with the living universe.

We are in a renaissance of herbal medicine with many plant teachers coming forth in this time to support human healing. As Jeremy Narby documented in his work with Amazonian shamans, indigenous wisdom keepers consistently describe plants as conscious teachers rather than passive substances. "The plants say they are the ones who teach," Narby writes, "and shamans are their students." This perspective invites us to approach plant medicines not as tools we use, but as wise allies with whom we enter sacred relationship—teachers offering their unique frequencies of healing to help humanity remember its place in the interconnected web of life.

Listening Yourself into Harmony with the Universe

As you attune to the living universe, you awaken the transformative power of Fire and the energy of the South. You call to the alchemical fires to burn away anything that isn't in alignment with your highest truth and listen your mind, body, and spirit into coherence with the living universe.

You come to recognize that the entire living universe is literally singing these frequencies to you in every moment. All that is required is for you to listen deeply and the reconnection will happen naturally—you don't have to "make" it happen. Author Robin Wall Kimmerer writes in *Braiding Sweetgrass*: "The songs are heard only when there is a place, and quiet time, and the listener has disappeared into the song." When you become that listener, dissolving into the melody of life, you find your place within it. And when you are ready, you sing back.

You may feel the weight of the world's brokenness and the urgency for change. But attuning to the living universe is not about fixing the world; it's about breathing and listening yourself back into coherence with the sacred symphony playing beneath the noise. In doing so, you become an instrument of harmony, resonating peace and love into the world. As Thich Nhat Hanh so beautifully says, "When we restore peace within ourselves, we can restore peace with the Earth."

Our lives are an ongoing, ever-unfolding process of listening ourselves into deeper relationship with the living universe. There is no final attunement. And the more you let go of needing to know exactly where life is taking you and be curiously open to the larger animate forces guiding you, the more room there is for wonder at the exquisite beauty of it all.

...

Essential Practices

Connect with the Heart of the Living Universe

Here, I weave together four practices—Heart Coherent Breathing, Central Channel Breathing, Non-Dual Awareness and Deep Listening Meditation—that have played an essential role in my journey. Together these practices guide you into deep attunement with the rhythms of life. Through breath, energy awareness, and deep presence, you'll begin to sync with the universal heartbeat, awaken your vitality, and open to a profound state of listening.

Step 1: Enter Coherence

Start by aligning with the heart's natural rhythm to create harmony within yourself and with the Earth's pulse.

1. **Find a sacred space.** If possible, sit beneath a tree, by a body of water, or anywhere in nature. If you're indoors, simply imagine yourself in a wild, peaceful place.

2. **Settle into stillness.** Find a comfortable seat—on the Earth, a cushion, or a chair. Let your spine be tall but relaxed.

3. **Rest your hand on your heart.** Close your eyes and take a slow, deep breath in for a count of 5, pause at the top for

1-2 seconds, then exhale for a slightly longer 6 seconds. Let your breath be natural, like an ocean tide.

4. **Call in love.** Bring to mind something that fills you with warmth—maybe the face of a loved one, a memory of sunrise over the mountains, or the gentle touch of a breeze. Let your heart soften and open.

5. **Breathe with intention.** Stay with this rhythm for a few minutes, feeling how your body begins to settle and sync with the universal rhythm of love.

Step 2: Awaken the Central Channel

Next, awaken your body's energy system and expand your awareness through the central channel.

1. **Engage your root.** Gently squeeze the perineum, like a subtle lift from deep within, activating the base of your energy system.

2. **Visualize your energy column and the torus energy field around you.** Imagine a stream of light running from the base of your spine to the crown of your head—like a golden river flowing upward and downward.

3. **Guide your breath.** Inhale, drawing this light up through your spine to the crown. Exhale, letting it gently flow back down, grounding you.

4. **Feel into it.** Continue this for a few breaths. At first, you may feel nothing, and that's okay. Over time, you might notice warmth, tingling, or a gentle current moving through you. This is your life force waking up.

Step 3: Enter Non-Dual Awareness

Now, shift beyond structured practice and simply rest in the open space of awareness itself.

1. **Notice awareness.** Instead of focusing on thoughts or sensations, gently turn your attention to the presence of awareness itself—the still, open space in which everything arises.

2. **Allow everything to be as it is.** Let go of any need to change, control, or engage with what arises. Simply rest in the knowing that you are awareness itself, boundless and free.

3. **Relax into presence.** If distractions arise, gently return to this simple recognition of being. There is nothing to do—just an invitation to rest as the effortless openness of awareness.

Step 4: Deep Listening to the Living Universe

Now, shift into a state of pure presence—open and receptive to the wisdom that flows through all things.

1. **Soften into silence.** With your breath steady and your awareness open, drop deeper into stillness. Let go of effort. Just listen.

2. **Be receptive.** The universe speaks in subtle ways—a feeling, a whisper in the wind, an image that arises within. Trust whatever comes, even if it's just the quiet.

3. **Rest in connection.** Stay as long as you feel called. This isn't about seeking answers—it's about being with life as it is, in its vast, intelligent presence. You belong to it all.

By blending these four steps—coherence, energy awakening, non-dual awareness, and deep listening—you naturally attune to the Heart of the Living Universe. Over time, this won't just be a practice, but a way of moving through life—awake, connected, and in rhythm with the greater whole.

...

Enhance Your Practice with Tuning Forks

The above practice is meant to be a complete practice. That said, with the addition of tuning forks, you can assist the body and mind to harmonize with natural frequencies. There are many incredible ways to work with tuning forks—here are some of my favorites:

Harmonizing with Nature's Perfect Fifth (C & G)

The C and G tuning forks produce a perfect fifth interval—one of the most harmonically balanced and stabilizing sound combinations in nature. This interval not only forms the foundation of many musical traditions but also mirrors the natural resonances found throughout our environment. The perfect fifth is celebrated for its ability to synchronize the human body and mind with the rhythms of nature, supporting a state of deep alignment and coherence.

Benefits:

- **Enhanced Brainwave Coherence:** The resonant frequencies promote clarity, focus, and deep relaxation by aligning brainwave patterns.

- **Nervous System Regulation:** They help shift the nervous system from a state of stress to one of calm and balance.

- **Natural Resonance & Grounding:** Mirroring the intrinsic harmonics of nature, these frequencies facilitate a deeper connection to the natural world, effectively synchronizing our energy and promoting overall well-being.

Using these tuning forks can be a powerful way to harmonize your inner state with the natural world, reflecting how the universe's own frequencies support our health and balance.

How to Use: Hold the C fork on one side of the head and the G fork on the other, approximately 3-6 inches from the ears. Strike them gently and allow their combined resonance to create a binaural effect, supporting deep mental clarity and energetic balance.

...

417 Hz & 528 Hz: Transformation & Heart Activation

417 Hz is associated with clearing negativity and breaking old patterns, while 528 Hz, often called the "Love Frequency," is believed to assist in cellular regeneration and DNA repair. When used together, they create a powerful field for healing and emotional transformation, and their combination generates a binaural beat of 111 Hz, a frequency found in numerous sacred sites like the Great Pyramid, and linked to heightened intuition and deep energetic alignment. Exposure to this frequency has also been found to deactivate the prefrontal cortex, reducing language center activity and shifting brain dominance from the left to the right hemisphere.

Benefits:

- 417 Hz helps dissolve negative thought patterns and subconscious blockages.

- 528 Hz supports heart coherence, emotional balance, and self-love.

- 111 Hz (Binaural Effect) enhances meditative states, cognitive function, and spiritual awareness.

- Together, they enhance healing processes, promote creativity and flow, and recalibrate the body's energy field.

How to Use: Hold the 417 Hz fork near the temples and the 528 Hz fork near the heart, or place them on either side of the head to create a binaural beat effect of 111 Hz. This practice can help align your emotional and energetic field, bringing greater harmony to the mind and body while deepening states of relaxation and insight.

…

The Sonic Slider Tuning Fork (93.96 Hz)

The Sonic Slider (93.96 Hz) is the 12th harmonic of the Schumann Resonance, designed to support your physical and energetic body in reaching a state of coherence.

Benefits:

- Encourages biofield resonance, aligning the body with natural harmonic frequencies.

- Supports cellular rejuvenation and increased vitality.

- Helps release tension and bring balance to the nervous system.

Steps for the Sonic Slider Routine:

1. **Begin by Striking the Tuning Fork:** Hold the Sonic Slider by the handle and gently strike it against a soft surface, like your palm or knee, to set it into vibration.

2. **Move the Fork Along Your Body:** Place the vibrating fork near key areas of the body, such as along your spine, heart center, or areas where you feel tension or discomfort. Allow the vibrations to resonate, breathing deeply as the tones move through you.

3. **Use My Guided Video for Support:** If you're unsure how to best use the Sonic Slider, follow along with my guided video on YouTube, which provides step-by-step instructions on using the tuning fork for optimal effect.

4. **Spend About 7 Minutes Daily:** Using the Sonic Slider for around 7 minutes a day can significantly increase coherence and vitality in your body, harmonizing your system to align with the Earth's resonant frequencies.

This practice can be a wonderful addition to your daily routine, enhancing the effects of other practices by bringing coherence and vibrational harmony directly into the body.

13
Allow the Flow

WEST – WATER

*"The cave you fear to enter
holds the treasure you seek."*

– Joseph Campbell

At some point in your journey, you must face your shadows. The direction of the West is here to teach you how to embrace your shadows and face your fears through the element of Water. There is no substance on Earth more cherished than water. Water gives life. Water cleanses. Water restores. Water heals. Water teaches us to meet life with acceptance and flow.

In the 1800s, settlers came to California seeking gold. As their hunger intensified for this precious substance, they used hydraulic mining—spraying vast amounts of water against mountainsides, forcing them to yield just a few small nuggets of gold. Millions of gallons of water were redirected, pushed, and blasted, forcing the Earth to release her buried treasure.

There's a powerful metaphor here. We push and strain to reach our goals, believing that heroic effort is required to bring us the metaphorical gold we seek. Nature shows us another way is possible.

Water doesn't push mountains; it flows down them. Freely, joyfully, water tumbles down the slope, polishing stones and carving a path effortlessly. In the same way, you can surrender yourself to the flow of life. This is the easeful way. The joyful way. The way where you don't have to try so hard, where you don't have to force water to strike the mountain. Instead, you let water flow over the sand and reveal the gold—naturally, peacefully.

The West invites you to accept and surrender—to trust the flow of life already carrying you down the river. Are you willing to pull up your oar and let her guide you? Chinese Taoism is an entire spiritual path based on surrendering to flow as Nature's way. In the Tao Te Ching, ancient Tao master Lao Tzu said: "Those who flow as life flows know they need no other force."

If you are used to working hard for what you believe in, I understand completely. In my case, I was working endlessly as a conservationist to try and heal the world. Given the state of the planet and humanity's ills, life felt like a constant struggle. Nothing seemed like it would ever be okay. No amount of work I did would ever be enough.

Buddhism describes this kind of suffering as being caught within the wheel of samsara—the cycle of dissatisfaction and seeking externally for happiness. I was looking for happiness outside myself, therefore no amount of doing would ever find a conclusion—an end.

Paradoxically, the answers came not through struggle, but through giving up my resistance to what's here. I had to stop trying to fix everything "outside" of myself and open my heart to accepting life as it is—and myself as I am. This wasn't easy, as every fiber in my being wanted to say "no" to all the awful and terrible things happening on the planet. Over and over again, I had to face the place inside that said, "No, I don't want that," and meet it with curiosity and compassion.

I had to drop my resistance and learn what it means to let life be as it is, without pretense—just like nature. Nature is always right here, showing you the way through the essential qualities of water—surrender and flow. Water has no resistance—it moves gracefully, adapting to whatever it encounters. To embody this wisdom, you must let go of clinging to and desire for specific outcomes. As spiritual teacher and author Adyashanti says, "Enlightenment is nothing more than the complete absence of resistance to what is. End of story."

Yet how do we actually embody this absence of resistance? How do we move from the forcing energy of hydraulic mining to the natural flow of water finding its way? The answer lies in trust.

Trust: The Bridge to Flow

Trust is the bridge to flow. Yet for many of us, trust feels elusive because we've learned to rely on control instead. Lack of trust arises from a deep-seated need to manage circumstances to ensure everything turns out okay. The controller in me was formed by early experiences that taught me: to be safe, I must control life and fix everything—because if I don't, who will?

The spiritual path taught me that to move out of despair and into an empowered place of trust, I had to go into fear and sit with it. As counterintuitive as it felt, I had to stop trying to fix everything "outside" and be willing to do the brave work of going within.

As teacher Blaise Kennedy said to me once, "I run to the pain like a firefighter runs into a building." That's where the juice is. That's where the problems get worked out. So, I had to drill into myself and root out the fear and distrust—to let this part speak to me and allow myself to cultivate compassion for this hurting part. I discovered many hidden pockets of sadness buried underneath the fear, and each time I went to root it out, the miracle was that softness, compassion, and love arose to meet the grief.

Leading trauma expert Thomas Hübl calls these stored energies the "crystallized past." What we experience as trauma is actually the unhealed, unintegrated energies surfacing to be released. Hübl describes it this way:

"Trauma is a response of the nervous system that becomes crystallized at the very moment in time a shock or adversity occurs, a kind of physicalized snapshot of the body-mind that is then stored in the body until it can be processed and transmuted... The undigested past desynchronizes us, limiting our ability to connect deeply with others, to achieve flow states, or to download emergent future light."

Energetically, the crystallized past is vibrations of tension held within the body as shame, guilt, anger, hate, and sadness. Until released, these energies will continue to color the present and limit your ability to respond from a fresh, uninjured place. It's why it may feel like you are carrying the past with you wherever you go. Because you are.

At the same time, you are a powerful being who is not bound forever to the traumas of your past. Through energetic and somatic practices, you can release these energies. You can rewire the patterns of sorrow, pain, and grief to self-love, compassion, and forgiveness.

Paradoxically, to let go of pain and difficulty, you have to go into it. You must courageously, boldly, deeply *feel* it somatically, asking questions like "Where is this pain in my body?" and then taking time to sit, be present with it, and listen. Let yourself feel into it. Does it have something it wants to say?

As you allow the pain to be seen and felt, you begin to integrate it. You have stopped moving away from it, and rather moved into it. Like an old wound that you ignored and was festering in the shadows, feeling is the doorway to clean the wound and release it into the light.

When you do, you allow the love that is always here—and that you are—to be revealed.

Embodying Flow

By allowing the flow of subtle energy in and outside the body without resistance, you are becoming embodied—you are growing the capacity to actually be more present and available in the world. You are, in a sense, waking up by waking down.

By dropping resistance to what is, you are allowing greater flow of energy in the body, increasing your body's capacity to embrace all of life. Again, from Dr. Hübl: "The body-mind is a system with which I relate to others and to my world; it is my instrument. By developing the subtle capacities of my instrument, I learn to tune in—to hear, feel, sense and see—to any unresolved energies in myself or others."

Dropping resistance to the flow of energy through embodiment is a gateway to experiencing higher levels of awareness. You wake down to reclaim and awaken the natural healing intelligence of your body. By waking down into the body and sharpening perception to feel the flow of subtle energy within, you grow the capacity to heal yourself.

Disease and pain result from stagnant energy that is contracted and not flowing. The more conscious you become of the flow of subtle energy within the body and biofield, the easier it is to notice where it is and isn't flowing. The basic process for unsticking this contracted energy is first to become aware of it, and second to direct your gentle loving focus there, turning disorder into order, chaos into harmony.

Try This: Heart-Centered Awareness
You can try this right now. Look around you. Everything that you see, everything that you feel, everything you can touch or taste or sense in any way is what is here in this moment. There is no denying that.

Now drop your attention into your heart and feel around you from your heart. What do you notice? Can you sense the shift? Do you sense how the duality of thinking in the mind drops away when centered in the heart? If you do, it's because there is no duality in the heart—it's only in the brain. In this way, the heart is naturally in rhythm with the flow of life. It's our onboard hardware to access flow in every moment.

Dropping Resistance

The way to remain in the natural flow of life is to become like a radio, effortlessly allowing the flow of information, without resisting what is coming through. The great sages and wisdom teachers knew surrender as a key secret to life. It is implied in terms like "letting go."

Letting go is simply dropping resistance to what is. Most people spend a lot of time resisting life and wishing things were different. Resistance to life comes in many forms, from the very personal (wishing that I had more money, that my body size was different, that I found my beloved) to the global (wishing that we had a different president, that corporations would behave more responsibly, that elephants wouldn't be slaughtered for their tusks).

Whether you realize it or not, every time you don't like what is happening, you are resisting life. Your resistance creates a contraction of energy, a clamping down on the natural flow of life force energy through the body and its bioenergetic field. If you continue to stop the flow of energy long enough, you create pockets of frozen, dissonant, and unintegrated energy within the field, which eventually leads to disease.

For as much as you may want to let go, it can still feel painfully far away, like something that you desperately yearn to see but can't—like driving down a beautiful mountain road aware of the gorgeous scenery, but not able to see it because the windshield is frosted over. You know the vista is there, but you can't see it. The process of allowing is analogous to defrosting the windshield. When you seek out the deeply held pain and its stories and beliefs and bring love and understanding to the hidden parts, you are bringing the medicine that's most needed. Not a pill that covers up the hurt, but rather actual healing.

Coming Home to Your Body

I sense that most of us metaphorically left the building when we were traumatized in our childhood. In other words, we vacated our bodies because the various traumas that we endured as children—whether severe, mild, or somewhere in between—when not met with the appropriate loving and compassionate response, created a sense that it wasn't safe to inhabit ourselves. As such, we went up into our heads and disconnected from our feeling sense.

The solution is to remain embodied as we experience life. Michaela Boehm expresses the embodiment of our humanness this way in her wonderful book *The Wild Woman's Way*: "Embodiment is the process of becoming alive to the signals of our body. The awareness of the signal of the body can also be described as central recognition. Being with the full array of sensory and emotional perceptions—the sublime as well as the ugly—allows us to savor the full human experience body, mind, and spirit. Alive, open, and integrated."

Thus, allowing the natural flow of life is to stay awake as you relate to the world. Meaning that you stay in a state of calm, open receptivity regardless of circumstances, allowing feelings to arise, be noticed, and released. In this way, waking up occurs through embodied allowing within our daily lives, rather than the traditional method of sitting alone in a lengthy solitary practice.

On the global stage, there is great chaos and turmoil in the world right now, a mirror to our own inner pain and chaos. The fire is lit. The house is burning down. And great shifts are taking place. As Thomas Hübl reminds us though, "The mind and body are designed to radiate with embodied light. We are all meant to feel our own life force, to see through illumined eyes, to know ourselves as purposeful and alive." Thus, every experience we have is an opportunity to notice whatever pain arises and alchemize it into love and compassion.

The Treasure in the Cave

Joseph Campbell reminds us that "the cave you fear to enter holds the treasure you seek." The cave is your pain, your resistance, your crystallized past. It's the dark waters you've been afraid to enter. But as water teaches us, the way through is not around or over—it's into and through.

The treasure isn't gold you must force from the mountainside. It's the flow itself—the capacity to meet life with an open heart, to trust the current that carries you, to remain embodied and present no matter what arises. When you stop pushing against the mountain and allow yourself to flow like water, you discover that you were never separate from the treasure. You are the treasure.

The West has shown you the way: feel the feeling, drop the story. Trust the flow. Allow the waters of your being to move freely, washing away what no longer serves, revealing the love and light that have always been here, waiting to flow through you and into the world.

...

Essential Practices

Four Powerful Practices to Release Stuck Emotions

1. Feel the Feeling, Drop the Story

Don't underestimate the power of this deceptively simple practice inspired by Pema Chödrön:

1. Close your eyes and notice any feelings present.
2. Presence the feelings without judgment, dropping any story around them.
3. Allow the feelings to move through you fully, somatically.

Without the story to sustain them, emotions often dissolve quickly, like clouds passing through the sky.

2. What Are You Resisting?

Resistance holds pain in place. This practice helps you soften into discomfort:

1. Identify a physical sensation or emotion you are resisting.
2. Locate it in your body.
3. Sit with the sensation without trying to change it, allowing it to be exactly as it is.
4. Notice if the intensity shifts over time.

3. The Ultimate "I'm Lost" Question

In the fog of difficult situations, a powerful question can shift energy and bring clarity where it felt like there was none. Use this question when you are feeling lost to cut through mental noise:

What is the next most loving thing I can do for myself and others?

4. Live in Flow Meditation

This meditation connects you to the natural flow of life:

1. Sit quietly and focus on your breath, releasing tension with each exhale.
2. Drop your attention into your heart.
3. Expand your awareness to the sensations within and around you.
4. Observe the flow of life without resistance.

Feel the peace that arises when you let go and allow life to simply be.

For a guided version, visit inner-rewilding.com

14

Align To Your Wild Heart

NORTH – EARTH

"Let yourself be silently drawn by the strange pull of what you really love. It will not lead you astray."

– Rumi

Here we arrive in the North, its element of Earth, and the closing of the circle. Like the hero in Joseph Campbell's journey who returns from the underworld transformed, carrying the elixir of wisdom back to their community, you arrive at the North bearing the medicine of your journey through the other directions.

To align to your wild, authentic self is the final homecoming—the full expression of your soul song where your life becomes an effortless expression of your unique genius and gifts. In this element, you reconnect with your indigenous self—your wild, loving heart with a clarity of purpose and depth of heart that is magnetic to everyone around you.

The element of Earth offers stability and belonging. It anchors you in the present moment and is the birthplace of inspired action. The North teaches you to root deeply into who you truly are, beyond the stories and conditioning that have shaped you. North is the place of maturation and homecoming, where you embody the wisdom of the ancestors and elders who carry the remembrance of our sacred connection to the living universe.

Most importantly, North carries the energy of both death and transcendence—not escape from your humanity, but the death of false identities and the transcendence into greater consciousness while remaining fully embodied. Like the ancient oak that grows taller by rooting deeper, your consciousness expands as you become more authentically human.

Remember Your Indigenous Nature

A white woman "mutt," with European heritage strewn across many countries, I have always felt like an ancestral orphan. Without ties to specific indigenous traditions, I envied those who were raised with strong land-based traditions. As though if I had been raised in a Peruvian or Celtic village, I would have received the secret knowledge of these traditions to guide my way. I longed to become indigenous.

But the truth is that I am—we all are—already indigenous. The word indigenous means "original inhabitant." To embody your true self is to reclaim the wild, indigenous nature within you. Because we are human, indigenous wisdom is encoded within our cells. We have all the tools we need to come into harmony within ourselves and the lands that we live upon.

As Bayo Akomolafe says:

"You are already indigenous: There is no need to 'become' indigenous… Well, what if you never left? What changes when the anxiety of 'arriving home' or 'becoming indigenous' is replaced with a studious slowness and a curiosity about where you are?"

The simplest path to reconnect with the indigenous self is to simply slow down and tune in with greater reverence and curiosity to your essence—to become like an archaeologist on a grand expedition to excavate the sacred and mystical temple of your heart.

Your heart's temple may have been buried beneath centuries of metaphorical mud: stories of unworthiness, unresolved trauma, or beliefs like "I am not good enough" or "I don't know how to do this." But no matter how thick the mud is, your wild, indigenous nature cannot be "lost." It's always there waiting for you to reclaim it.

The Inner Rewilding practices—the meditation and inquiry of the East, the attunements of the South, the trust and surrender of the West, and the grounding of the North—are all ultimately pathways for connecting with your loving essence… in Rumi's words, "the strange pull of what you really love."

Within indigenous traditions, sacred ceremonies and rituals of song, dance, and prayer have also always been paths for connecting with our deep heart. These ceremonies open our hearts to come into rhythm with life—to feel the flow of the universal life force of love within—and when we do, we feel authentically, unapologetically ourselves.

The Sacred Death: Shedding What No Longer Serves

This recognition requires a kind of death—not of your body or humanity, but of the false stories about who you thought you were. Campbell understood that every true transformation requires the hero to die to their former self. In the North, you undergo this sacred death willingly, consciously.

Like the serpent that must shed its skin to grow, you must release the identities that no longer fit. The snake doesn't escape its snake-nature—it becomes more fully serpentine, more alive, more itself. This is the kind of transcendence the North offers: not escape from your humanity, but the flowering of your fullest human potential.

For so long, you've been shaped by the influences of your lineage—mother, father, ancestors—into versions of yourself that may not feel fully authentic. The conditioning wraps around you like old skin, and while it once served to protect you, it now restricts your growth.

Honor your heritage but remember that you are so much more than these inherited patterns. The serpent doesn't reject the skin it sheds—it honors what protected it while recognizing when it's time to let go. You can appreciate the conditioning that kept you safe while choosing to outgrow it.

This is the sacred paradox of the North: you must die to live, shed to become, let go to finally possess your true self. As you release what no longer serves, you discover that what remains is indestructible—your essential nature, your wild heart, your authentic self that has been waiting beneath all the layers.

The Return: Living from Your Wild Heart

By remaining rooted in your wild heart through life's joys and challenges, you can finally fall in love with the world as it is—and yourself as you are. No apologies. No need to fix everything before you decide to love it. The Earth isn't broken and neither are you.

You rise transformed, like the hero returning from the quest, carrying the treasure not for yourself alone but for the healing of the world. You act as the grand co-creator with the divine that you already are. You become the protagonist of your own story while serving the larger story of life itself.

Be gloriously here as you are—and let the Earth be here as she is. This is the ultimate teaching of the North: that transcendence and embodiment are not opposites but dance partners, that death and life are not enemies but lovers, that you can be fully human and fully divine at once.

This is love and what we are here for.

Essential Practices

Deep Earth Grounding

This simple yet powerful practice helps you establish a deep connection with the Earth, aligning your energy with its stabilizing rhythms. You can do this practice outdoors for a physical connection or indoors using visualization and intention.

Step 1: Find a Quiet Space

- Choose a location where you can relax undisturbed. Ideally, this will be outdoors—on grass, soil, or sand—but it can also be indoors with a comfortable seat or mat.

Step 2: Center Yourself

- Sit or stand with your feet firmly planted on the ground. If you're sitting, let your hands rest gently on your thighs. Close your eyes if you feel comfortable doing so.
- Take a few slow, deep breaths, allowing your body to relax with each exhale.

Step 3: Visualize Your Roots

- Imagine roots growing from the soles of your feet, or from the base of your spine if sitting. See these roots extending downward into the Earth, deeper and deeper, until they reach the rich, stabilizing energy of the Earth's core.
- As your roots anchor, feel the Earth's energy rising up to meet you, flowing into your body like a warm, steady current.

Step 4: Set Your Intention

- Silently or aloud, state your intention to connect with the grounding energy of the Earth. For example: *"I align with the Earth's energy and allow it to stabilize and support me."*

Step 5: Breathe and Feel

- With your roots firmly anchored, begin to synchronize your breath with the sensation of energy rising from the Earth. Imagine each inhale drawing grounding energy upward and each exhale releasing tension or chaotic energy downward into the Earth.
- Spend a few minutes simply breathing and feeling this connection.

Step 6: Optional Enhancements

- Incorporate tools like a sound bowl, drum, or essential oils like copaiba to deepen your experience. Gently strike or play the instrument, or diffuse the oil nearby, allowing its vibrations or scent to assist your grounding process.

Step 7: Return to the Present

- When you feel grounded, gently bring your awareness back to your body. Wiggle your fingers and toes, and take a final deep breath, expressing gratitude for the Earth's support.

Sacred Journaling

Let these questions guide you into the heart of the North's medicine — a place of belonging, strength, and inspired action in your own life.

1. What are the "breadcrumbs" that have been leading you back to your wild heart?

Write about the moments, sensations, places, and experiences that make you feel most alive, connected, and in love with the world.

2. If you could stand in your most grounded, sovereign self, what truth would you speak?

Explore what it feels like to live in alignment with that truth, and what stories or influences you might need to shed to walk it fully.

3. How does the Earth teach you to love as you are, right now?

Describe how you can root into the present moment, embracing both your humanness and your divinity without waiting for yourself—or the world—to be "fixed" first.

...

Dream Your Future into Being

What is your wild heart calling to create through you? If you were living in full alignment with this heart, what would your life look like?

To dream your future into being is to align deeply with your creative heart and allow it to guide you. Your wild heart already holds the vision of your soul's purpose—it is simply waiting for you to listen.

Start by giving this heart a voice. Create a vision board filled with images and words that resonate with your deepest truth. Before you choose the elements of your vision board, spend intentional, quiet time in nature. Let the Earth, the wind, and the rhythms of the natural world awaken your creative imagination. Allow your heart's whispers to rise through meditation, walking, running, or however you most easily receive guidance.

As you connect with this creative force, drop the stories of what your mind thinks would be a good idea. Let go of what you "should" want or create and instead focus on what feels deeply true in this moment. What lights up your heart? What stirs your soul? This is the raw material for your vision.

Your vision board is more than a collage of images and words—it is a sacred portal, a reflection of your heart's deepest desires and a declaration to the universe. Place it somewhere you'll see it daily, such as above your desk, your altar, or another sacred space. Each time you look at it, let it activate the path you are dreaming into being.

15
Homecoming

"When you learn to love and let yourself be loved, you come home to the hearth of your own spirit... You are no longer outer-directed and other-directed, you come home to yourself and learn to rest there."

– *John O'Donahue*

One of my most beloved teachers, who has a way with words like no other I've ever known, is the late Irish poet and philosopher John O'Donahue. O'Donahue weaves the ecological with the philosophical—the wildness of landscapes with the tenderness of the human heart—as a restoration of belonging, a spiritual homecoming to oneself and the world.

I feel this homecoming journey is the essential human journey of rewilding—to restore our connection with the living universe, the infinite field of cosmic intelligence that moves in all things.

Through this intimate reconnection with the living universe, we gain everlasting nourishment—nourishment that cannot be depleted or extinguished and comes from a well that is always overflowing. We sit humbly at the feet of something much greater than ourselves. Like a hearth for our wandering souls, the living universe becomes our true mother, welcoming us in from the cold with a warm fire, soup, and bread, and she has room for every part of us—all our fears, our grief, our laughter, and our joy.

The definition of home is a place to rest and replenish. Home brings a feeling that all is well and a sense of fundamental belonging. We come home so we can rest. We come home so that we can regenerate. We come home to be in harmony with the rhythm of life and ourselves, because as O'Donahue proclaims, "When you are in rhythm with yourself, you are untouchable."

This journey taught me that my love of wild places and pain at their destruction was actually my soul crying out for connection to this living universe—to feel her rhythm, harmony, and order, but also her grace, acceptance, and joy. It was never just about saving wild places.

The bridge that allows us to cross over the river of our pain to the meadows of joy is self-love. And the gates of self-love are opened by reconnecting to the living universe—to the divine, or, if you prefer, the nature within. Because when we do, we see that all along we have been held by something much bigger than us.

In retrospect, I realize that I didn't know what self-love really was, despite my decades on the spiritual journey. All those layers of self-judgments—I am not good enough, smart enough, beautiful enough—were keeping the gates firmly shut. I wasn't conscious of that, really, at the time. All I knew was a deep unsettledness and agitation.

Right now, there is great agitation throughout our world. A pervasive sense that we cannot rest—that we must do more to fix the planet and to make our world safe—an unrest that comes from our disconnect with nature.

Our failure to feel connected to the living universe has roots that go far back to ancient Greece. There, philosophers like Plato and Aristotle planted the seeds for our modern disconnect when they saw nature as something to be controlled or shaped through human intervention. Later, Descartes wrote that through science we could become "masters and possessors of nature." Such thinking set in motion a legacy that fueled the scientific and industrial revolutions, allowing humanity to view nature as a commodity to fulfill our desires, rather than honoring our intrinsic connection to the living universe.

Many articulate voices are emerging to challenge humanity's "mastery over nature" paradigm. In his book *Intelligence in Nature*, anthropologist and author Jeremy Narby writes, "The evidence points to intelligence being a property of the living. Our relationship with nature must change from domination to dialogue, from seeing nature as a mute object to recognizing her as a subject that speaks."

Robin Wall Kimmerer in *Braiding Sweetgrass* says: "In the Western tradition, there is a recognized hierarchy of beings, with, of course, the human being on top—the pinnacle of evolution, the darling of Creation—and the plants at the bottom. But in Native ways of knowing, human people are often referred to as 'the younger brothers of Creation.' We say that humans have the least experience with how to live and therefore the most to learn—from plants and animals."

Suzanne Simard says: "The scientific evidence is showing that trees are not simply the source of timber or pulp, but are part of a complex, interdependent circle of life. We must move from thinking of ourselves as masters of nature to participants in it."

One of the great 20th-century theoretical physicists, John Archibald Wheeler, a colleague of Albert Einstein and the one who coined the term "black hole," said: "We live in a participatory universe."

The chorus of academic voices urging us to shift our view of nature from mastery to participant-ship is growing louder. Narby, Kimmerer, Simard, Wheeler, and many others like them are the new thought-leaders of our times. It's time to redefine our relationship with nature as one of collaboration and co-creation.

This reunion with nature is our true homecoming. Through it, humanity will, in the words of Pierre Teilhard de Chardin, discover fire for the second time: "The day will come when, after harnessing space, the winds, the tides, and gravitation, we shall harness for God the energies of love. And on that day, for the second time in the history of the world, we shall have discovered fire."

As ancient humans have been doing for millennia, but which for a short time we forgot, we are finding our way back into conversation with the living universe. And because we live in a musical universe operating on the principle of resonance, we are being invited to sing. Nature is always singing us home. And all we need is to sing back to her. Sing to her our heartache and grief. Sing to her our celebration and joy. And in doing so, we complete the cycle. We join the dance of this great mystery of life.

Everything in the external world is a mirror. As the saying goes, "We see the world as we are, not as it is." When all is said and done, the journey home is not so much about preserving the wilderness outside us as it is about remembering what we already are—nature in all her wildness, alive within us.

Go then. Rewild yourself. Excavate your true heart from the shadows and let it sing out your soul's song—the sweetest song ever sung. Then, whenever the light grows dim, let that song be your beacon—your unyielding call that announces again and again your glorious place within the grand community of life, saying: *Yes! I am wild. I am free. I am home.*

Acknowledgments

Every book is a collaboration. From my earliest counselors at Camp Tawonga to the many teachers, guides, colleagues, friends, and family who've shaped me—each of you supported the birthing of this book in your own way.

I offer deep gratitude to the place where this journey truly began: the Shambhala Mountain Center (now Drala Mountain Center). Shortly after, Stephen Altair and Kevin Schoeninger invited me into the inaugural Raising Our Vibration cohort—a 10-week immersion that changed the course of my life. To them I am eternally grateful, as well as the dear friends I met through this community.

To my lifelong friend and teacher Stephen Altair: you found me at a moment of deep unraveling and became a beacon of light, guiding me from the chaos of my mind into the radiance of my heart. I remain forever in your deepest debt of gratitude.

To the spiritual teachers who have illuminated my path—Blaise Kennedy, Rupert Spira, Loch Kelly, Moojibaba, Adyashanti, John Prendergast, Dr. Jeff Tarrant and Richard Rudd—thank you for your profound wisdom and presence. Your teachings will always live in my heart.

Immense gratitude to Dr. Jeff Anderson, whose wise counsel guided me through the challenges of mold poisoning and on the road to recovery. Thank you to the teachers and staff of the Human Potential Institute and especially my dear friend Lindsey who mentored me through fasting and the many crazy things I experimented with in those early biohacking days.

In January 2021, I began studying breathwork with Julia Mikk. Her encouragement and enthusiasm for this book were the spark that lit the flame. That very week, I said yes to writing it. I am eternally grateful for her support and the profound breathwork teachings she offers. Deep thanks also to the loving cohort that journeyed with me, especially Mel Finnerty.

To the gifted teachers who opened my ears and heart to the healing power of sound and frequency—Eileen McKusick, Jonathan Goldman, David Gibson, Paul Hubbert, and Jeralyn Glass—thank you for helping me tune to the harmonies of the unseen.

To the jungle and the Master Plants who shared their wisdom with me—thank you. And to the lineage holders who steward these sacred traditions and invited me to learn: Lindsey, Josh, Andre, Katherine, Elio, Taita Juanito, Taita Luis, Mama Juanita, and Ima. I honor you.

To my Lander sweat lodge community and the stewards of the lodge, Bill Boycott and Joanne Orr—thank you for the sacred space you held during a time of great transition. You helped peel away the layers, both literal and metaphorical, that no longer served me.

Thank you to the staff and board members at The Nature Conservancy and the University of Wyoming. I honor you for your devotion to protecting our planet. Special thanks to Paula Hunker, my first mentor and dear friend at The Nature Conservancy—you were a guiding light when I was just twenty-something and getting my feet under me.

Immense gratitude to all my dear friends for your friendship, for the mountains we climbed, the passes we crossed, the ceremonies, the song circles, and the soulful conversations along the way. I love you all.

To my dear friend Kathy Browning, who left this Earth too soon—I love you, and I thank you. Your spirit walks with me still.

To my sweet and gifted publicist and dear friend, Nina Kaiser—thank you for introducing me to Nicola Humber and Unbound Press, and for weaving resonance into every step of this journey.

To all the incredible souls at Unbound Press—especially Nicola Humber, whose visionary energy sustained me in moments I thought I couldn't go on, and to my thoughtful editor Jesse Lynn—thank you for your support, insight, and belief in this book.

To my Norwegian family, Arnulf, Irene and Monia, I have never forgotten your kindness to take me in as your own daughter/sister for an entire year and make me feel so truly welcome and loved. Thank you.

To Scott, my faithful partner through many beautiful years in Colorado and Wyoming—thank you for the life we shared, the daughters we raised, and the nature we loved together.

To my parents and close family—there are no words that adequately express my gratitude for your steadfast, loving support. Your belief in me has been one of the greatest blessings of my life.

To my dear soul friend "Green Man" Gregorio—thank you for listening patiently, reading drafts, and offering gentle feedback. Your devotion and friendship have meant the world.

To my daughters—your very being reminds me that love is boundless. Just when I thought I'd reached its depth, you showed me there was more. You are beauty, you are love, you are truth, you are radiant. Anything less would be a lie.

And finally, to the unseen realms—my tree, plant, and animal spirit teachers, the ancestors, the angels, and the invisible threads of grace that guided every word—I bow to you in reverence and wonder.

Resources for Inner Rewilding

Personal Offerings

Inner Rewilding Meditations, Courses & Retreats
Explore my guided meditations, 1:1 and group programs, and nature-based retreats.
https://inner-rewilding.com/

Teachers & Practices in Subtle Energy, Meditation, and Non-Dual Awareness

Stephen Altair & Kevin Schoeninger – Subtle Energy Meditation & Raising Our Vibration
Foundational teachings in subtle energy awareness and heart-based living.
https://raisingourvibration.net/

Rupert Spira
Teacher of the direct path and non-dual awareness through the lens of Advaita.
https://rupertspira.com/

Loch Kelly
Guides in effortless mindfulness and glimpses into awake awareness.
https://lochkelly.org/

Blaise Kennedy
Contemporary teacher in non-dual realization and embodied awakening.
https://blaisekennedy.com/

Moojibaba
A spiritual teacher sharing Advaita Vedanta through presence and inquiry.
https://mooji.org/

Adyashanti
Spiritual teacher offering teachings on awakening and true nature.
https://adyashanti.opengatesangha.org/

Breathwork & Somatic Transformation

The Solignment Institute
Transformational breathwork journeys and teacher training programs with Julia Mikk.
https://solignment.com/

Meditation, Frequency & Coherence Tools

Muse Headband
This was the game-changing device that provided neurofeedback support when I was learning to meditate. Visit my website for a link to purchase Muse and receive product discounts. https://choosemuse.com

Biofield Tuning
Explore tuning forks, sound healing, and recorded sessions for vibrational alignment.
https://www.biofieldtuning.com/

HeartMath Institute
Science-based tools and techniques for heart-brain coherence and emotional resilience.
https://www.heartmath.org/

NeuroMeditation Institute
NeuroMeditation is a brain-based approach to the practice of meditation.
https://www.neuromeditationinstitute.com/

Wisdom Teachings & Personal Growth

Richard Rudd – The Gene Keys
A transmission of living wisdom rooted in contemplation, astrology, and transformation.
https://thegenekeys.org/

Sacred Plant Medicine Retreats

The Nature Within
Plant medicine retreats devoted to healing with the wisdom of plant spirits and Earth connection.
https://www.thenaturewithinus.com/

Aya Healing Retreats
Ayahuasca retreats rooted in Shipibo lineage, offering deep healing and integration.
https://ayahealingretreats.com/

About the Author

Holly Erin Copeland is a former ecologist turned guide to the wild within. Through Inner Rewilding, she creates sacred containers where frequency, ceremony, and presence converge—helping spiritual seekers and earth-conscious leaders return to the peace of their true nature and the wild joy of being human.

With decades of spiritual practice, a background in conservation biology, and training in Biofield Tuning, Neuromeditation, breathwork, and ceremonial guidance, Holly weaves science and mysticism into a path of deep remembrance and belonging—to ourselves and to the Earth. She now lives among the oaks and pines in the foothills of California, where she can still be found trail running and contemplating the beauty of this wild, precious life—and delights in watching her daughters, Mia and Abby, chart their own wild paths.

Learn more at inner-rewilding.com

www.ingramcontent.com/pod-product-compliance
Lightning Source LLC
Chambersburg PA
CBHW020412080526
44584CB00014B/1288